Midlifeman

Midlifeman

A BOOK FOR GUYS
and the Women Who Want to Understand Them

Larry Krotz

Canadian Cataloguing in Publication Data

Krotz, Larry, 1948–
Midlifeman : a book for guys and the women who
    want to understand them

ISBN 0-7710-9589-9

1. Middle aged men.   2. Middlelife crisis.   I. Title.

HQ1090.K76 2000   305.244´081   C99-933003-9

We acknowledge the financial support of the Government of Canada
through the Book Publishing Industry Development Program for
our publishing activities. We further acknowledge the support of the
Canada Council for the Arts and the Ontario Arts Council for our
publishing program.

Typeset in Bembo by M&S, Toronto
Printed and bound in Canada

McClelland & Stewart Inc.
The Canadian Publishers
481 University Avenue
Toronto, Ontario
M5G 2E9

1 2 3 4 5   04 03 02 01 00

for Stephanie

CONTENTS

Foreword

BY CAROL SHIELDS

"In my late forties," Larry Krotz writes, "I've entered the silly season of a man's life."

Silliness is an opportunistic disease; it strikes us – men and women alike – in our transitional phases when our physiology is shaky and when our fragile arrangements are open to question. How to behave, what to wear, what lines of inquiry are political suicide? – the old guidelines are exhausted, and, suddenly, there are no gender models to help us to become good citizens of the contemporary world.

A few years ago I sat down with my old friend Larry Krotz for an earnest discussion. I was writing a book, which was to become *Larry's Party* (no relation, despite the name), and needed to know what it was like to be a man at the end of the twentieth century. Larry had some answers for me, but also his own set of questions. What was the new comportment for forty-year-old men? He was twice married, twice divorced, the father of a teenage daughter, a man with an interesting and variable job and a wide circle of friends. What should a responsible man be thinking about at his age? What should he be *doing*? The bookstores are filled with how-to-be books for women, but very few that address the modern man.

In this gentle, wide-ranging book Larry Krotz turns his attention to fatherhood, to friendship, to the traditional male symbols of cars and cigars and Super Bowl Sundays. He investigates his role as a lover, as a writer, as a caregiver to an elderly parent, as a citizen of the world. He worries about his changing body, about his life history which left him uniquely without role models. And, of course, he worries about mortality and its linked question: what, after all, is the point of a man's life?

Ultimately, this is not a book about male silliness, but about the natural confusion that men face in a rapidly changing society. Larry Krotz's thoughtful reflections provide a perfect guide to the new millennium.

Introduction

The house lights dim, and the spot picks up a lone, shambling figure coming out to the middle of the stage in front of his band. Applause swells. Bob Dylan. As he begins his set – "Tangled Up in Blue," "Highway 61," a heavily stylized version of "My Back Pages" – a couple of kids, maybe twenty, twenty-three years old, one of them tall with a knitted Bob Marley–style hat covering his dreadlocks (though he is a white kid) stand up in their seats and start to groove. There has been some smoke, everybody can smell it, and they are a little blitzed. But they love what pushing-sixty-year-old Bob is singing. They want to dance. Arms wave, bodies sway. At the other end of the row of green-zone seats high up in the

I

hockey arena where I'm sitting, a trio of young girls do the same. Really dance.

They are, the five of them, exceptions. Most of the audience who've just heard Joni Mitchell and now are settling in for Dylan are my age. Or older. Hair betraying that first touch of grey, muscle tone struggling with the urge to slacken. Or bodies left looking (that awful word) paunchy. Many of us wear glasses. A lot of the people around me are couples who hold hands, bent on remembering, keen for nostalgia. But twenty-five or thirty years of extra life has also put us somewhere else. "Sit down," somebody shouts at the dancing boys. "Please sit down," chimes in a female voice. The kids pay no attention. Maybe they can't hear; the music is loud. Not quite rock-concert ear-splitting, but with a drummer and three guitars, it's up there. The bald guy in the row in front of us who, when the warm-up band played really loud had his hands clapped over his ears, clenches his fists and mutters something first to his wife and then to the people sitting behind him. His view of the stage, about fifty metres away, is now completely blocked. He picks up an empty paper cup, crumples it, takes aim, and fires it at the boys who are three or four rows in front of him. He misses. The paper cup loop-the-loops and lands on the head of some confused person far below. The bald man scowls. A couple of his friends pat him on the back in commiseration.

A fellow in our row gets up. He's wearing a suit jacket, but has accessorized it for the occasion with a dark blue shirt and psychedelic tie. That aside, he looks like he might be a psychiatrist with a practice at the children's hospital. "I'm going to get someone," he says as he squeezes past us in the dark. He means an usher, security. I have to smile. Joni Mitchell's last number, twenty minutes ago, was about the Woodstock Nation. The Woodstock Nation, now grown up, older, and greying, is going to resort to authority.

Which is, I guess, a better option than using violence. But a far cry from the other option: joining in the dance.

I feel, suddenly, quite old. I know I'm not old. Not really old. But, certainly by association, I am something that I didn't used to be. I'm on a bridge and I'm fast passing from one side of it to the other. I'm not the dancing kid. The woman sitting beside me is not a dancing kid. Although we try to be wry about it, every minute we are quietly sliding, like water flowing to its level, a little more into the other group, the group that has a whole different agenda and a whole different view of things.

I am a middle-aged man; a man now well into my forties. A midlifeman. I'm living through what I enthusiastically believe to be the best time of my life. But I also know, especially at moments like this, that it is a time of change. Some of this change is quiet and creeping, almost imperceptible; other aspects of it are dramatic and speedy. All of it is wedded to this time of life, an imperative of passage and progress that has taken me, as it has my contemporaries, and wrenched us out of our individuality, placing us into something called a "time" or a "decade" or a "generation."

In the fifth century B.C., Confucius made a schedule of a man's life that, 2,500 years later, rings contemporarily enough that he might have concocted it last week. At age fifteen, according to the Confucian dictums, we must devote ourselves to learning and study. At thirty, we ought to work independently. At fifty, achievement at the highest levels of ability should be evident so that, at sixty, we receive applause and awards. At seventy our ultimate reward is to have become free to do whatever we please.

But what about forty? Oddly, in the middle of the list, the master left out what is possibly the most important decade of all. The forties is a kind of keystone decade without which, surely, the preparation of the early years makes no sense and the satisfaction of the later ones is not possible. If achievement at the highest levels of ability is to be evident at fifty, a great deal of pressure is on for the preceding ten years. By forty, our life enterprise should be well started, but the final results remain far from certain. It is half-time in the locker room, but not the time to rest. In almost every way it is a make-or-break time; it is already too late to allow the kinds of mistakes that at a more precocious age we could have recovered from, yet it is far too early to coast. It is an urgent time; all our early lives we want and crave and lust after things, but something, perhaps a sense that this is our last kick at the can, makes this the decade of the most urgent of all our wanting. It is the time of the most poignant desire, the most greedy craving, yearning, lusting. I know a man, never married, whose vow early in his forties was that he would have a wife by fifty. He did not succeed. It is a frightening time, the most difficult and perhaps, therefore, the most exciting decade of all. The decade of the forties is a bridge. Though we might want the kids who are blocking our view to sit down, we can still go to a Bob Dylan rock concert.

For the better part of a decade, I've been a man in my forties. In the course of my work and my life, I have dealt with hundreds of men in their forties. Many of my friends are men in their forties. Men in their forties have always been the people to emulate. The people whose actions, creations, and decisions affect all of us in so many ways – actions of government, decisions in education or in business, initiatives in publishing and communications and entertainment are in a huge, disproportionate part taken by men in their forties. For years I have looked up to men in their forties. For years I have listened to the musings and complaints of women who try to deal with and understand men in their forties.

It's a cliché, I know, to refer to life as a journey. But each decade is in fact that. My forties has clearly been a journey, some of it taken by the seat of my pants. In retrospect, I realize that I hadn't really any grand plan for the itinerary. Consequently, the trip has been full of surprises. Some were delights; some were things I wish I'd known ahead of time.

This book is in part a memoir of the journey. It is also a reassessment. If the forties are one's middle age and I am at mid-stage in my life, then this is a good time to reassess the rules and the assumptions I (and others) have been operating by. This is a time to look at problems and consider changes. I am intrigued by how we reinvent ourselves and, sometimes, how we fail or are prevented from reinventing. Sufficiently intrigued to put my observations down on paper. This book is about what it is like for men to be in our forties, but it is also about the world, as seen through the eyes of men in their forties. And it is a very particular world, this late-twentieth-century Western world at the swing of the millennium, governed as it is by television, airplanes, credit cards, computers, news disseminators, and information overload.

One of the things a man must come to terms with in his forties is his limitations, the first of these being his mortality. I've tried, as I've watched my forties speed by, to understand my very ordinariness. But I have had, on the other hand, the good chance and the luck to encounter some extraordinary people and some extraordinary opportunities. This book is also about those.

1

Passing the Age of My Father

Midway on our life's journey, I found myself in dark woods, the right road lost.

— D A N T E

On June 12, 1997, at about nine o'clock in the evening, I became older than my father. I passed the age that he was when he was killed in a car crash while I was still a boy. He would never grow older than his father who lived, vigorous and healthy, to eighty-eight. But here was I, suddenly, as old as he. And then, a minute later, older. Now, no matter how long I live, I will always be older than my father.

It's strange to be older than your father; it is a perversity of nature, like being your own grandpa. It is not simply the change of generation shoving history forward; what lay ahead for me was unknown terrain – a landscape my father did not live to explore. What I was to learn also was what a tricky passage it can be. And what things I would be forced to confront while making the passage.

Some years ago, in a magazine, I came upon an essay by a man at middle age whose father, then elderly, had just died. His point, which he pushed strenuously, was about the freedom he felt upon the death of his parents; a bittersweet freedom to be sure, but nevertheless a liberation that he believed would turn him loose from all the things that had inhibited him until then. He would no longer bear any requirement to prove to, to answer to, to please the parent. And this meant for him, he thought, that now he could do anything he wanted. Our parents, particularly our fathers, deeply affect our motivations, our systems of excuses, and, doubtless, our freedoms.

But freedom, for me, was hardly the issue. The issue was rather a set of questions, questions I'll perhaps spend the rest of my life struggling to answer. As best I can word or pose them, they are these:

- What happens to you when you reach the place where, in age at least, you actually transcend your parent?
- What does it mean to be a man?
- How do we learn to be men?
- And, finally, do the times we live in now make it more difficult or less difficult for us to be men?

Passing the age my father was when he died took me past another milestone, as well. Throughout my early life I kept in the back of my mind an ideal age. I'm not quite sure why, but I seemed to require a number or time as a reference for everything. Something that would provide an image of what I might be growing into or an idea of what I was heading toward. It was an arbitrary age at which I believed I would be at my best, an age I secretly imagined as being "prime," when I would be at the top of my game. Everything tracked toward that. The magic number was a year in my late forties. For a long time, it never registered on me that this ideal age was the same age my father was when he died.

So when I passed the age of my father I also passed the age I had all my life thought of as being ideal for myself. Now, suddenly, I felt doubly in no-man's-land. I had no useful idea of what my father would have been like as an older man, and I had no conception of what I ought to be like either. I had no creation of my own imagination to look forward to and no model to guide me.

Now that I am older than my father, everything about my memory of him has changed. The need to remember him has changed. My ability to remember him has changed. One lasting memory is of lying on my stomach on the kitchen floor when I was nine years old, my skinny arms trying to match the push-ups of this awesome, older, bigger man. But now I am not nine. It is impossible in any usual sense to remain the son of your father when your age passes his. When I was a teenager, even though my father was dead, he served as a kind of guide, a mentor functioning through the memories I had of him as well as through the legend of him, which grew up quickly after his death. His legend was polished and assiduously tended to by my mother, and it sat, an icon of no small stature, within what remained of our family. "Dad would be proud of you," my mother would say, using "Dad" as a name. This in itself made him more real and present, as if he were waiting in the next room and would at any moment come through the door to express his opinion in person. Or she would say, "Dad would like to see this," not even the conditional "Dad would have liked to see this." He was present, he was wise. His judgement was impeccable, his record unblemished. Any shortcomings he had as a human being, a husband, a father, a man, were lost in the revisionism that being dead awarded him. He could be the infallible anchor for his adolescent sons despite his absence. Or perhaps because of his absence.

After I became an adult and moved away from the rural community where I had grown up, I would go back there. I would drive over bucolic back roads to the little immaculately kept cemetery where my father is buried. Across the fence, cows grazed beyond the shade of maple trees. On the gravel side road a farmer, somebody I might have known, trundled by on a John Deere tractor or rattled past in a pickup truck. Birds swooped among the trees, and the full, green, waxy leaves shimmered in the breeze. My father was in the ground, beneath the polished rose granite of his stone, surrounded by a century's worth of my ancestry – aunts and uncles, grandparents and great-grandparents. But although I knew he was in the ground, I felt him in the air, somewhere over my shoulder, as if he were taking in the scene with me; not imparting anything direct, but there nevertheless.

But now that I am older than he, it is as if my father at long last is truly dead. His relevance to me has altered dramatically. To seek advice or assurance now, even from his memory, would be to seek the counsel of a younger man. And that makes a huge difference.

What have I become in all this time? Well, like many men, I have amassed a substantial assortment of the trappings that help define what and who I am. I have been a husband, though I am not one now. I am a father though my daughter has, in the blink of an eye, all grown up. I have what you might call a career, though not so much of a career as, say, someone who has a career in banking or a career in teaching or a career in television. I have travelled to a number of far-flung places. I have made a little money; I have spent most of it. I have owned houses and fixed them up, but now I don't own anything that you could call property. I have paid taxes, voted in elections, worked on a couple of campaigns on behalf of candidates I thought I should feel happy to have represent me. I have owned two Labrador retrievers. I have enjoyed a number of friendships. A few of those I have moved on from, too, or have seen them move on. But I am graced to have more left, certainly, than I started out with.

Yet here I was, momentarily at least, without a map. You reach the darkest part of the forest, the narrowest, most forbidding section of the road, and astoundingly your chart gives up. Close to my desk I keep a collection of maps, my favourite being a late-nineteenth-century outline of the continent of Africa. It is largely blank. There is detail along a narrow band marking the coast. Over Egypt and what is now South Africa the information gets a little more dense. But the vast middle is empty, and carries two labels: "Unexplored Territory" and "Negroland." It is charming as an object, but useless to depend on to get somewhere. I now possessed double the freedom longed for by the essayist in the magazine article; I had no father, I had no memory of a father at my stage of life. Yet those freedoms seemed – at least momentarily – overwhelming. I was on my own. I was disconcerted. There's no shame or weakness, I realized, in wanting a guide; even Dante needed Virgil. Yet here was I, all by myself in Unexplored Territory.

One day I tried to think about the world my father lived in, as if I might find something through the comparison. He lived through the Depression. He lived through the Second World War. These were dramatic, extreme times. The first was an era when, no matter what you did, nothing seemed possible. In the second, everything was turned – by Hitler, Churchill, Roosevelt – into either black or white, good or evil. Then my father lived through the next decade and a half of the post-war years when, with peace, prosperity, production, everything, miraculously, seemed as possible as twenty-five years earlier it had been impossible. I was just emerging from the gym after a particularly sweaty workout. One thing I know my father's world did not include was aerobic workouts in the company of tyrannically fit thirty-five-year-old women wearing neon tights and Lycra thongs. It also didn't include change rooms where the men at the next lockers discussed going to Aspen for Gay Ski Week. In the times in which I live, everything seems neither quite possible nor quite impossible. And I think of nothing as being either black or white.

Sometimes, were he here and were I to try to explain what the world looks like to me, I fear my father might find it hard to understand what it is that puzzles us men at the turn of the twenty-first century. What makes us feel so much at sea, like so many pieces of driftwood banging against the shore? The security of our identity, of what it should be to live as a man, seems elusive. Behind our practised bravado and careful façade lurks the unmistakable hint of hesitation, the eye that won't quite hold the gaze. My father would have presumed that his children were going to be the luckiest people in all of history: comfortable, convenienced, no need to work with our hands. He would have been befuddled by the uncharted state we seem to find ourselves in.

In our time, men appear to have lost that heroic something which, in one form or another, sustained our gender for at least three thousand years. We don't have full-blown heroes now, only compromised ones. Or anti-heroes. Scientific studies as well as anecdotal evidence show a demoralization of men that comes off, to say the least, as sad. The most widely watched characterization of middle-aged man is Homer Simpson. Two popular and widely discussed movies in the last few years have had as their subject the humiliation of men. The male characters in a nasty movie called *The Company of Men* humiliate themselves by behaving abominably. The heroes of the Oscar-nominated British film *The Full Monty* scrabble to salvage a humorous dignity out of their diminishment. Neither story offers a very cheery view. Both films portrayed men as needing a come-uppance, or receiving a come-uppance. Women cheered in the cinemas where I was. Both films presume that men should not open their mouths because what will emerge is bound to be wrong.

On one level you could say that the problems men face now are paltry; we don't have Hitler or the Depression or even the Cold War any more. But our compass is wobbling. We look around to see if there is anything convenient to blame. Maybe women; there is always that primary temptation to blame women. The progress of feminism has left men eating dust; its energy and power, its moral imperative and even its purchasing heft has changed the world. But instead of a happier world for everybody, it can be argued (and has been) that female empowerment afflicts the male of the species. Studies tell us that it is boys who are now failing at school, and furthermore, that they are to be blamed for it. When girls fail the system is blamed; when boys fail, it is their own fault.

Perhaps we could blame Einstein. Or Freud. Since Einstein and Freud there can no longer be any absolute standard, we are told. There can be no God-figure or absolute truth. For the traditional idea of men, particularly the notion of father, the demise of the absolute has been devastating. Our traditional idea of the father (for better or worse) is linked with our idea of God, so when we don't have a very strong idea of God, the edifice of the father wobbles as well, and threatens to come crashing down.

Then we wonder whether the malaise might have any number of other causes. Perhaps it's due to the affluence in which we live. Not only affluence, but an affluence that comes to us, on the whole, quite easily. We feel we haven't been tested. Our generation's overriding myth is one of working incessantly and competing furiously. Yet I know of no agreement on the prize or the purpose. We live comfortably, yet we would live comfortably even if we didn't compete furiously. Our competition is about something else. Of all my friends who strive and work hard, few understand themselves to be part of a race that is worth the price of their individual efforts. The problem, perhaps, is that we have not been able to join in and be part of some collective dragon-slaying. That's it! We're afraid we haven't had the chance to be "real men." We fear we are soft, and that depresses us. We live under the curse of comfortable times that make us think of ourselves, even when we are exhausted, as somehow lazy and unproductive. Football on television and Promise Keepers or Million Man Marches do not fill the void. Relative to men in other times, we fear we might be less. Masculinity, as Camille Paglia labels it, is "the most fragile and problematic of psychic states."

Or maybe all of this is what it has always been. A difficult passage, a tricky threshold. An appallingly inadequate and haphazard way of moving into what will be, ever so briefly, the moment when the world is ours. Maybe all men in all generations have felt this unease. "Nobody really knows his own father," Homer has Telemachus say in *The Odyssey*. Since Odysseus, the father, had been absent fighting and wandering for more than twenty years, Telemachus had reason to say what he did simply on the face of things. But a broader interpretation is that we find our fathers not by encountering them per se, but by coming into our own identity. By becoming comfortable men ourselves. Maybe we now are not unique. Maybe my father would have felt all of this too, had he got that far.

Finally becoming older than my father ought to have made me, like the fellow in the magazine essay, enormously free. It ought to have left me alone and unfettered on a playing field where I had as much of an opportunity as I would ever have to make the rules myself. Instead, it made me feel vaguely guilty. Not guilty in the sense that I had done anything wrong, but guilty in the way a student might feel when he realizes that even though he has had all the time in the world to study and prepare, he isn't quite ready yet to take the test. Webster's dictionary defines guilt, along with "the fact of having committed a breach of conduct," as "a sense of inadequacy." Being older than my father makes me feel that I should also be, somehow, wiser. Older and wiser. I must protest that I'm not. I have it no more together today than I did last year. Or the year before that. But it never mattered before; it never seemed to matter that I be wise (nor was there ever any pressure) until I came to the anniversary of my father's death. The anniversary that said objectively, the guard has changed.

The countryside where I grew up remains a world totally different from the cities where I live. Recently, I went off to re-explore the fields and woods that were part of the farm owned by my parents when I was young. A creek of rippling clear water, shallow enough to wade through, still bisects a forest of old-growth maple, beech, hemlock, and cedar, a finger of what was once known as the Queen's Bush (Queen Victoria) when my ancestors and others from Europe came to settle and clear it a hundred and fifty years ago. I pushed through calf-deep mid-December snow, climbed gingerly over fences of rusted barbwire, and negotiated a still-unfrozen cedar bog. Eventually I found myself far enough into the woods that I could no longer hear any sounds, save those of the forest, no whine of snowmobiles, no rattle of cars from the road or tractors from the farm. Just birds, jays and crows, and the wind soughing through the towering hemlocks and bending the winter maples. I looked at animal tracks, hare and fox.

I tried to summon memory and presence. The woods were filled with the ghosts of my father and his father. And on the next farm, my maternal grandfather. I looked for signs of their labour: a pile of rails now rotted into the ground, a tangle of sheet metal that had been the roof of a sugar shanty that once sheltered the spring boiling of maple syrup. The log footbridge my father built to ford the creek was gone. Much had changed. It had been twenty-five years since my last walk through there. I looked for favourite trees from when I was a boy and found some eventually, though I became disoriented and lost looking for them. Many of the big old trees had been logged or had fallen from age or in wind storms. And the rest had changed. The forest had been fenced from cattle and let grow. And grown it had. A new generation of maples, now twenty years old with a diameter of six inches, obscured much of what I remembered.

The world my father nurtured has been logged over. But it has recovered in new growth. And that world has been passed on to me. This is the way we inherit the world. The kid in the schoolyard taps you on the shoulder, "You're it." *It.* I don't remember that we ever stopped to contemplate the meaning of that little one-syllable word. Suddenly, you're it. And the world passes, not just physically, into the hands of the next generation, but psychologically it becomes theirs as well. This elemental passage is more profound than previous adult passages, such as the first time you voted or your first job or the first time you paid taxes. More profound even than setting up, for the first time, your own household and family. It is different, too, from having your parents die. It is the possibility, held however briefly, of having the world on no other terms but your own. There is no point resisting; it is as inevitable as the change of the seasons or night following day. The new team taking the field is you. You are handed the ball and you mustn't whine; you can only gratefully accept it.

2

My favourite place on earth is a flat shelf of black, Precambrian granite that slopes gently into the bracing clear waters of Lake of the Woods. The exposed part of my rock is level enough to set a chair on when I want to read in the morning, and smooth enough to lie on, flat on my back, when I want to stare up at the dance of the aurora borealis that almost every night after midnight visits the late summer sky. Millions of years of scrubbing by water and wind have smoothed and shaped my rock, except for a fissure, right up its middle, caused much more recently by a shiver of the earth or, more likely, by water again; a minute expansion of ice. The crevice is still sharp-edged; you could cut your finger on it. Covering the plane of the rock are other soldiers in the ongoing war among the elements, the war to transform, to break down, to claim. Platoons of lichens form a miniature, pale green map, and out of a couple of lesser fissures spring goldenrod and a small cedar tree. The poor cedar has been deformed into a tragically stooped crone by the west wind that funnels persistently up the long bay.

Lake of the Woods sometimes doesn't seem to be a proper lake; only at its south end is it a broad expanse of water. Elsewhere it is deep bays and heavily treed islands – bays and islands, bays and islands, like cul de sacs in endless pattern. Its watershed is north of the Mississippi and west of Lake Superior. All that it gathers flows, eventually, a great distance north to Hudson Bay. Minnesota is to the south, Manitoba is across to the west, Ontario is behind me.

Up a gentle hill, beneath a couple of towering white pines and against a brace of cedars, is my cottage.

I've been going to this place every August since 1984. And each time, the first thing I do, even before unloading the car and putting the milk in the fridge, is walk down to the rock and stare out at the lake.

Loon Cottage is the smallest of a family of pine-log cottages built in 1939 and 1940 around a main house named, charmingly, after the loons that fill the bay: Laughing Water Lodge. Loons are a kind of bellwether for a lake, a sign of its health. If loons come to a lake, the lake is okay. I've read that places in New England are ecstatic to have loons, after many years absence, returning to their lakes. Lake of the Woods is full of loons.

The people who run Laughing Water Lodge, Rob and Barbara, are teachers who used to live in Kingston, Ontario. But one day they packed up everything and came here, where they found jobs at the school on the nearby Indian reserve, Onigaming. This is their investment, their project, their retirement dream. I actually have seniority here, because I'd been at the place already for one summer before they purchased it. Consequently they pretend to defer to me, which is nice. Our little joke.

It's a simple cottage. A bedroom, another room with a pull-out couch and a basic kitchen, and a screen porch that runs the width of the front, facing the lake and the western sky. When a storm comes it blows rain for a couple of hours straight through the screen and I have to mop up with towels, and with anything else that will soak up a deluge. Then the sun will re-emerge and a brisk wind will skitter the clouds past and all will be wonderful again.

"I'd paint the floor blue. Or yellow," says Jane, the woman I've been seeing for a couple of years. She's scrutinizing the wide pine boards that are now just varnished dark wood. "And then you could have white wicker furniture." Jane likes to settle in to a place, put a stamp on it. She's a whiz at decorating; she knows how to make everything look just right.

I remind Jane that I don't own the cottage. Though sometimes I pretend that I do. Nobody else, in my fantasy, pays rent for it, nobody else uses it, nobody else sleeps in the bed or enjoys the view in quite the same way either from the screen porch or from the rock at water's edge. Nobody else listens as appreciatively to the loons.

I pick up my binoculars, Bushnell 7-15 × 35, to focus on the island where the eagles nest. I peer across a quarter-mile of water to a dead white pine that stands above the other trees of the island like some awesome skeleton. Sure enough, on their gnarled perch, the pair of bald eagles I see every summer are ready to make their regular late-afternoon hunt.

My daughter and her friends come up the hill with a bucket full of crayfish. Crawdads. They lure them with pieces of hot dog tied to fishing line on the end of a stick. And when one of the crustaceans takes the bait, the girls jerk the line, dancing around excitedly until they can decide who will have the chore of touching it and putting it into their pail of water. Then they don't know what to do. They bring them to Bob, who with his wife, Linda, rents the cottage next door every year at the same time that we're here. Sarah's friend, who has come with her from Winnipeg, is Rachel; Amy and Kate are Bob and Linda's children. The girls are adolescents now: Sarah and Rachel are twelve, Amy is thirteen, Kate is eleven. In the city they experiment with nail polish. But here, suddenly, they forget about both urban and adolescent pressures. They run down to the dock or to the rock and they catch crawdads.

Sarah was seven when we first came out here. This was our slice of the summer, what we had after she'd had her other vacation with her mother. Laughing Water Lodge. Loon Cottage. Some years ago, our dog, Daniel Boone, expired here of a heart attack brought on by old age and a hot summer. We buried him up the hill by the power-line cut, placing some flat rocks to mark his grave. Now we always pause respectfully when we pass nearby.

The other cottages are rented by people from Winnipeg or from the States. Bob and Linda and Kate and Amy come all the way from Omaha. Including a ritual stop in Hibbing, Minnesota, so that Linda can pay tribute to Bob Dylan, the trip takes them two days. When they get here, the girls pick up where they left off the August before. Bob goes out in his boat to do a little fishing and to paint views; Linda sits on the screen porch — not as nice as mine — and reads the pile of books she's brought with her. At night we get together to drink Canadian beer and play Trivial Pursuit. The girls form their own team.

Jane goes back to the city, and I am left with Sarah and Rachel. I set up my typewriter on the table in the screened porch and get to work. I am writing a book about Indians. Not the kind of Indians who live in Bombay, but the kind, like Norman Copenace, who live down the highway at Onigaming, where Rob and Barbara teach. I've been researching it and travelling all over Canada and now it is time to write.

The girls lounge on the lumpy leather couch that has suffered too many rain storms. It is cracked and faded, but it retains for the girls its cottage comfort. Their long, skinny legs stick out over the arms. Duke, Barbara and Rob's brown retriever, noses against my door. Duke is getting old and crotchety and doesn't warm easily to the numbers of people who come and go from this place; but I get along with him fine.

When I want a break, I take my folding chair down the hill to the rock and sit there, looking out over the lake. This is the oldest rock in the world, formed three billion years ago, which is quite something when you think that the earth itself is dated at about four and a half billion years. I'm reading *Arctic Dreams* by Barry Lopez – which I think might be a model for my book about Indian reservations – and the book *Family Resemblances* by Lowry Pei, who is a relative of the famous architect. I'm also reading the Song of Songs in the Bible.

The summer has been dry; all the grass is brown. I throw pots of water on the dead clumps at the foot of the cottage steps to see if I can turn them green. Several spruce trees are dying, infected by budworm; the white pines look thirsty. Drought brings in disease and insects and gives all of this devastation free rein. Nature's way. Then, in the proper scheme of things, there would be a fire and life could start afresh. We humans find these cycles disturbing; we want our surroundings to look good; fires frighten us. But the lake is okay. Though you can see that its level has gone down. A family of mergansers tool their way around the base of my rock. Seven ducklings swimming with confidence. I watch the fishermen from Totem Lodge, the smart lodge filled with well-heeled Americans on the other side of the bay, go by with their Indian guides. The Indian guides are going to be the heroes in my book.

3

When Your Friends Run the World

___

One of life's more sobering moments is when you realize that the people you went to high school with are running the world.

I don't mean to imply that I know the people who are *really* running the world, the people who all by themselves supposedly can make decisions that – should they wish – can turn the ship around. I don't get to have lunch with Kofi Annan or the chairman of General Motors. But some of my friends have become the first mates, allowed to steer the ship so long as it stays its present course. They are substantial cogs in the machinery that gets things done, serious players in the world of the moment. Some of them have become reasonably heavy hitters.

I find it remarkable that I should know such high-powered people. But what is even more remarkable is that these people, as I remember them, should have become high powered. When I first met them, we were in high school. In high school, what you know, what you cultivate and appreciate, is the worst and the weakest side of your friends. These are friends whom I liked and still like immensely. But it would never have occurred to me to trust the future to their hands. We enjoyed each other's foibles too much; we liked to think of one another as dorks. The world, we thought, was run by people who were unusually wise and had their heads on straight. They were not like anybody we knew; our friends were capable of weaknesses and stupidities. You would never want them to have real responsibility, let alone power.

Recently I've seen four different people with whom I went to high school. This is what these old friends do now: David owns a business with offices in three cities and sales in countries all around the world. In the last few years he has resisted buyouts that would have netted him several millions of dollars. John is the assistant managing editor of a big-city newspaper. He has mastered computer and printing systems that weren't dreamed of when we were students, and is in charge of continually making over production methods and keeping up with the latest technological developments. Donna, after first becoming a social worker, went back to school to study law and now is a chief prosecutor for a large district. Donald is a civil servant. Always political, he sublimated his partisan side and is now able to work with governments of all stripes. He sits in a comfortable office and has extensive responsibilities for health-care policy.

So the most dramatic change to the world over the past ten years for me has nothing to do with new inventions or technologies, the Internet, global warming, or the end of apartheid in South Africa. The biggest change is to my internal view of things, which comes from noting where my friends have landed and the substantial positions that are suddenly held by people I know.

I could make my list longer. Another Donald used to curl up on the floor of his room and, inspired by the wildlife stories of Farley Mowat, experiment with canine sleep habits. Every hour and a half he would wake, turn around twice, and then lie down again. Norman played hooky from school at least one day every week so he could either sleep or go skiing. Terrence acted out Ernest Hemingway fantasies and made everyone who came to see him put on boxing gloves, then tried to give them a bloody nose. Bob used to place realistic rubber turds carefully on the floor at the back of history class, hoping to dismay the teacher: "Look, sir, what somebody did!"

Sleep-on-the-floor Donald and rubber-turd Bob are both now judges. Skip-school Norman, a respected member of the geology department of a large university, has become an expert on certain formations of cretaceous rocks, and gives papers all over the world. Terrence, the boxer, eventually became a prominent writer.

Others I did not know so well, but who were still schoolmates, have gone on to become the manager of the Stratford

Festival, head of the National Banker's Association, and minister of defence. The other day in the business section of the newspaper I saw the name and picture of a woman I remember from economics class – where she obviously took better notes than I. She was listed as being on the boards of directors of six major companies.

I realize that whether my friends are competent to run the world is not really the issue. Rather, it is that the moment power and responsibility pass into the hands of people you know, your attitude toward that power undergoes a revolutionary shift. No doubt it's always been like this. In every generation from the beginning of time, whatever community responsibility and power there has been has had to be passed into the hands of a younger group; Neanderthal hunters doubtless experienced a transitional moment when their sharpened sticks were picked up by the next generation. It's just hard to get used to the idea that power is passing to people you recall from gym class. Which is also something that has always been the case: somebody went to high school with Henry Kissinger; somebody went to school with Hitler; somebody went to school with Alexander the Great, Shakespeare, and Thomas Jefferson. But that was then. Now there are people my age who remember gym class with Bill Clinton and Bill Gates.

Realizing that the world is being run by people I went to high school with, or people like them, has taken the mystery out of power and authority for me. It has turned that Cadillac into a Chevy. Maybe, like those members of my parents' generation who remained stubbornly supportive of "the Presidency" through the last years of Lyndon Johnson and even through Richard Nixon, I don't really like this. I'm ambivalent about whether I welcome this demystification. It is always more comforting the other way, like having your mother tell you when to go to school. Now we all have to be both more vigilant and more responsible; the emperor has no clothes.

Two things I notice about my friends. One is that they have become very hard workers, a lot more tenacious and diligent than I would have expected from the signs they gave in their earlier lives. A couple are classic workaholics, defining themselves by their jobs. Others simply recognize they have no choice but to work like donkeys if they are to maintain their positions in a world where someone else would bump them, given half a chance. Like long-distance runners, they apply themselves over tedious hours in very disciplined ways. John goes to the newspaper at nine in the morning and considers himself lucky if he can return home by ten at night. When we have lunch on a Friday, he tells me he will work on Sunday and that this is no exception, he works weekends all the time. David lugs a fat briefcase when he comes home for dinner. After a couple of hours with his family and helping to put his two young sons to bed, he goes to his study and gets back to it. He is usually in his office on a Saturday or a Sunday unless he has to use the weekend to fly to Vancouver or Europe or Asia. I play tennis with Donna on a Sunday morning. After our match we enjoy a pleasant, lingering lunch. But then she says she must get going, she has work to do to prepare a case that starts on Monday. In each instance personal life exists in a delicate balance with the career, the role, the job. Donna has never married. Donald is single and gay. John and David are both on their second marriages, with young children. Everyone is alert to how the busyness of their work affects the other parts of their lives. "Life is flying by," complains John. "My son is growing quickly and I hardly catch the moments."

Something else I note is that my friends have become – for lack of a better word – conservative. Winston Churchill warned not to be too liberal in youth for fear of becoming too conservative with age. I am driving across town with David and his wife on a dark, drizzling November night. At stop-lights we are descended upon by squeegie kids, the freelance windshield cleaners that Mayor Giuliani outlawed from New York and that Toronto law-and-order types have set their sights on. David shoos them away (we are in his car) and starts to rant. I'm surprised. I'm always surprised at the vehemence of reactions to the squeegies as opposed to, say, those who are outright panhandlers. I would have thought such entrepreneurial effort would have impressed David; the squeegie kids are staying off welfare, after all. Besides, this is the David who, when we were nineteen, disassembled the furniture in the bedroom of our student apartment so that he could sleep on the floor with a spear he'd brought back from Ethiopia. David, who had a wild tangle of red beard back then, is not so unconventional now. "Have you considered what those metal studs on their jackets and jeans would do to your paint job?" he demands.

"The squeegie kids frighten me," says his wife.

Of course, my friends are more conservative now because they have more to conserve. When you become a property owner and car owner and furniture owner, you want safe neighbourhoods and clean, well-kept streets. You want good municipal services; you want efficient and effective police. When you have kids, you want good schools. You have a vested interest in law, order, and good government.

But there are more reasons to be conservative. My friends who are doing well feel they must preserve the system that we live under – the banks, the government bodies, the education and legal systems that make up our society – because these are the systems they work for; the ones that made them prosperous and prominent.

So don't remind them that when they were in university in the 1960s and 1970s they talked about revolution.

If you remind me that once upon a time my generation talked about revolution, I won't get angry. I'll just wince with wry amusement and perhaps a twinge of guilt. Part of the wince will be an acknowledgement of how silly and herdlike it was of us to use the R-word in the first place; we hardly knew what it meant. What did we want, dressed in our army surplus fatigues? Did we really imagine hiding our preppy asses in mosquito-filled ditches like Che Guevara, while soldiers patrolled the highways? What did we expect to do next?

But the other half of the wince comes from comparing the lives we have now to the rhetoric we spouted twenty-five or thirty years ago. This is when I am ashamed of how far short our achievements have fallen of the ideals we once held. Do we even remember those ideals, or have they been replaced by our portfolios? Concern for community has been replaced by worries about the economy and, for whatever combination of reasons, not much is about to change. We're going to stay the present course. The Davids among my friends are for tax cuts; Donna makes sure we have law and order. I don't think we lack compassion, but we have changed. We have become protective of the established order; we *are* the established order. The most vocal anti-establishment revolutionaries at my college are careerists now in the tax department.

With the exception, perhaps, of the victories of feminism, which got Donna her high-placed job, what is to show for the idealistic crusades of our youth? One great victory of our youth was the loosening of sexual mores, but nobody seems to be reaping much in that area these days. Family and position, or perhaps simple lack of time and energy, mean that Kissinger's adage about power as an aphrodisiac doesn't seem to get much of a try-out. Not among my friends, at any rate. Instead of such pleasure-based preoccupations, everything leans toward work. We have working lunches and working dinners. Exercise is a "workout." Travel, whether by air or car, tends to be frenzied and stress-filled. We have invented a cult of "busyness" in which it is a matter of pride (and a symbol of status) to have our time booked months in advance and (more perverse) to be able to complain of some stress-related disorder.

Seen in the light of our lofty expectations, the world in the hands of my generation might seem a massive disappointment. We are more materialistic and probably less spiritual than our parents ever were. Conspicuous consumption reigns. The young scribes from the alternative or student presses who urged us comrades to the ramparts in the sixties now work for business publications, do pop pieces in *Vanity Fair* to celebrate the lifestyles of corporate merger kings, or produce books advising on mutual funds. We have neither saved the environment nor made a hint of a mark on the vast and growing discrepancies in distributions of wealth. We don't believe very strongly in collective action; the only thing we support about government is that it should shrink. Our attentions are consumed by pensions, retirement savings schemes, and frequent-flyer reward systems. We believe in the "family of man" only so far as we support global transfers of capital, global markets, and unfettered trade. We like speedy airplanes to get from one place to another, and speedier transfers of currency over computer networks. We want smoother passport and visa clearances when we go as tourists or business travellers into the Third World and all the while we uncensoriously watch foreign aid to those places shrink. We believe in supporting culture with mega-buck contracts for sports, media, and entertainment stars. We love our leather-upholstered sport utility four-wheel drive vehicles and seem oblivious to the horrific pollution and urban sprawl our car culture breeds. There are fewer hospital beds, fewer schools (and of worse quality), less community, less charity, probably even less goodwill than our parents left us.

I'd love to be able to look the next generation in the eye and say, "Yeah, the world is a better place. We had our chance and we've done something wonderful with it. We had our principles and we didn't deviate from them. Consequently the world's wealth has been equitably redistributed, poverty has been eradicated, and the environment is safe for at least the next three hundred years."

I can't say that.

Yet we have not dropped the ball. The world is still turning round.

It's not malevolence or unbridled greed that is alone responsible for our failures. Power is a nebulous quality. From the outside, it seems something monochromatic, undiffer-entiated, singular. From the inside, it's not nearly such a tidy entity. You wake up one morning and someone points out, "You've got power." And you answer (a bit startled), "I do?" This is not to say that a small group of people on the earth do not possess enormous disproportionate wealth and privilege and should have done something with it. But it's easy at the same time, easier now than when I was looking at the world from the other side at age twenty, to see why we haven't. Working from day to day entangles us in a net of what is immediate. We get mired trying to function inside a nuanced problem, having to agonize over and balance competing goals, conflicting values, overlapping entitlements. We are in charge of things, but we are still woefully ordinary people with painfully ordinary visions and painfully ordinary weaknesses.

Which is both the problem of the world we inhabit. And the beauty.

It is disconcerting to think how easily, almost imperceptibly, people end up in control of things. As Woody Allen pointed out, showing up is ninety per cent of the secret for success. If you are in the right place at the right time (and belong to the right group), some form of power is not that hard to attain. That's just the way it is.

Though not everybody got there. Not long ago, when I was visiting the small town where my mother lives, I ran into a guy named Frank. I didn't recognize Frank at first, partly because he looked about a hundred years old. The years had not been kind. But once I figured out who he was, I also remembered that Frank had been the class bully. If some weaker boy was going to be thrown fully clothed into the showers after gym class, chances were Frank would be leading the charge. Now Frank wasn't so fearsome; he looked like he lived in some place with a mean dog, and car parts strewn throughout the yard. But no real power. I was secretly pleased to note that he hadn't become the attorney general.

But do the rest of us know that, like Frank's power to throw more hapless members of his class into the showers, such power as we have is transitory? The people of my generation have yet to suffer the sort of anti-establishment assaults with which we dissed our elders in the 1960s and 1970s. We have got off lucky. We are the people, remember, who once loudly proclaimed that it was not possible to trust anyone over thirty. Now we are long past thirty. So far, generations X and Y, the baby-boomer echoes, our own children, haven't come after us. How long can that last? Perhaps a dissing is coming for my contemporaries in high places. We are vulnerable; I wonder how we will react.

4

Ambition: The Itch a Man Can't Scratch

How does thou wear and weary out thy days
Restless Ambition, never at an end!

— SAMUEL DANIEL

Ted was having lunch with his closest male friends. Of the four men in the shaded courtyard restaurant – too early yet to be crowded – three were lawyers. Ted is a lawyer. This was a critical moment for him, and once the waiter delivered the tray of Heinekens and took orders for Caesar salads and grilled-chicken sandwiches, all joking, that holdover-from-high-school jocularity that happens whenever men, no matter how old, get together, stopped. We knew this was important. Ted cleared his throat as if calling a meeting to order.

It had been a well-guarded secret kept even from most of his friends, but at last it was common knowledge that Ted had had a long-standing affair with a woman from his work. Four years; a long time to pull off a secret life. But it was now over. The usual shit had hit the fan; he had confessed to his wife, dropped the woman, eaten humble pie in his family and his community. And now Ted was thinking of his future. He wanted to use these friends to test out his possibilities.

It was apparent he was restless, unresolved; not very happy or fulfilled. There was a big hole in his life, a gap where, for forty-eight months, so much of his focus and energy had been directed. Not only sexual energy, but also the enormous energy required to maintain a dual life and a deception. He should have been exhausted, but he wasn't. He seemed the opposite of exhausted: primed with energy and eager to plough into new fields. He wanted and needed to do something dramatic and dynamic. He was addicted to the adrenaline and he was also, at forty-three years old, aware that you are only offered the podium once. Action was, in his mind, called for.

It would have to be important action. This was one of those forks in the road where the choice determines everything about how the rest of your life will turn out. Ted approached the matter carefully, like the lawyer he was. He was severely earnest, almost tense. "The way I see it, I look at my life and I have two choices," he said, placing his palms flat on the table as if each well-manicured hand were holding down one or the other of the choices. "I leave my wife and resume an affair or something with Catherine – maybe even marry her. Or I forget Catherine, go back to my wife for good, and" – brief hesitation – "go into politics." He wasn't smiling. He was serious. Ted had always been interested in politics and was known to be well-liked by the leadership of the party in power. If he could be kept untainted by scandal and surrounded by at least the pretense of an adoring family, he had a very good chance of a successful run for the legislature. The ensuing pause was, shall we say, pregnant. This was not the proposal anyone had anticipated.

The friends looked at one another. One of them, George, started to examine the bricks in the wall. Phil squirmed in his chair. Ted looked as if he wanted to say something more, but knew it was no longer his turn. The silence, though, was going to drive him crazy. Finally Phil spoke. Tentatively. A combination of things in him and in his life had provoked Ted into a moment of high ambition and it needed to be examined for what it was, and for what it could lead to. "Help me here," Phil ventured, "I want to be clear. As you see it, your options seem to be screwing one person or screwing the entire population."

Male ambition is many-headed beast, a hydra that is responsible both for most of what is good as well as almost all of what is bad in our world – perhaps in the whole history of the world. It is creative, it is aggressive, it never sits still. It produces incredible spectacles – from theatre to wars. It drives the engines of trade, of exploration, of discovery, and of government. It is responsible for the invention of the light bulb, central heating, the electric chair, and napalm. It has given birth to institutions as elaborate as the United Nations and Super Bowl Sunday. It drives men like Ted (not to mention

John F. Kennedy and Bill Clinton) to have affairs with women who are not their wives. And it drives them to enter politics. Male ambition is such an entwined mix of everything from altruism to vanity that it is exceedingly hard to untangle. It is both sorry and wonderful. Where would civilization be without it? But where does it come from? And why are we such slaves to it?

Frequently I feel a pull from its familiar urge. I want, I want, I want. Nothing I have is enough. Nothing I have done up to now is enough. The itch is overwhelming, like that irritation in the very centre of your back which you can't quite reach to scratch.

At such moments I know that my impulse and my desire is absurd, even ridiculous. Nobody is making me do anything to reach farther. If I am going to try to achieve more, for whom am I achieving? Will it make my family love me more? Who will care? If strangers should notice me, is there any real value in that? If some mark of mine is left after I'm dead and gone, of what value to me is even that?

Yet I don't ask these questions. I don't think, "I could make a living quietly and anonymously; I could live unobtrusively and modestly." In fact, such questions are so out of keeping with the male character that when men throughout history have occasionally posed them, we have made those men into saints. Hardly any man I know takes seriously Jesus' pronouncement, "Blessed are the meek." No, like others, I get the itch. And then I promptly rush headlong to indulge in another clench-jawed, impatient quest for some kind of triumph. I do so fuelled by the thought that whatever adventure this might be, it is the only chance I've got. Furthermore, I disregard any notion that I might get into all kinds of trouble.

Attempts to understand this thing, ambition, have led to endless speculations. Shakespeare's text is peppered with the word, either in reference to its follies – "I have no spur to prick the sides of my intent, but only vaulting ambition which o'erleaps itself and falls on the other," says Macbeth – or in reference to it coming up short, as in *Henry IV*: "Ill-weaved ambition, how much art thou shrunk!" Norman Mailer (certainly not immune to the bug himself) called it a psychosis. Forty years ago, in his essay "The White Negro" (*Advertisements for Myself*, 1959) he speculated how driven, aggressive, high achievers functioned outside "the mutually contradictory inhibitions upon violence and love which civilization has exacted of us." They must, thought Mailer, be low-level psychopaths, and he found the evidence everywhere. "The condition of psychopathy is present in a host of people including many politicians, professional soldiers, newspaper columnists, entertainers, artists, jazz musicians, call-girls, promiscuous homosexuals, and half the executives of Hollywood, television, and advertising. It can be seen that there are aspects of psychopathy which already exert considerable cultural influence." Author Raymond Tanter, in a discussion of recent political dictators (*Rogue Regimes*, 1998), poses the possibility that North Korean leader Kim Jong-Il was "a little frightened boy" lashing out at his father, whom he blamed for the death of his mother, and suggests that Fidel

Castro's motivation for his revolution in Cuba was "the secret knowledge that he was not a good enough baseball player to make the grade in the American major leagues."

Sometimes, among the more highly restless of us, achievement itself isn't necessary, only the preliminary thoughts about it and steps toward it. T.E. Lawrence, the First World War adventurer who became famous as Lawrence of Arabia, said of his great appetite, "When a thing was in my reach, I no longer wanted it; my delight lay in the desire" (quoted by Malcolm Brown and Julia Cave in *Touch of Genius: The Life of T.E. Lawrence*).

Somewhere there must always be a Darwinian explanation. The urges that drive us could be rooted in the fact that we've never really got beyond being cavemen. Ambitious, competitive behaviour springs from patterns deeply imprinted on our chromosomes. The psychological trigger could be a historical memory of competition from the days when men needed to beat out one another in order to attract fertile mates.

However, I believe this male ambition is a more complex matter than simply competition between males. It is not just a jostling with your buddies for a comparatively better position. It puts a man up not just against other men, but against everything. It is not comparative, but absolute. Like golf, male ambition is frequently a game played primarily against yourself. Once you've tired of pitting yourself against your contemporaries, you must still go up against the large abstractions of time, energy, mortality, the expectations of your parents (living or dead), and the huge picture of history. Ted's desire for a political career – and probably for his affair – had much more to do with his need to assert himself against himself than it did with any competition with another man or men. Rather than label it ambition, it might be better to call it appetite, or greed. It is a deep hunger. "An ardent desire for distinction," rules the Oxford dictionary.

Whatever it is, and wherever it comes from, it seems to climb in pitch through a man's thirties before causing him extreme torment in his forties. A few years ago I encountered a thirty-six-year-old man who was midway through realizing his ambition to swim across fifty of the major rivers of the world. He was a nuclear physicist in Rotterdam. But I met him in northern Canada, on the shores of the surly-looking Nelson River where, in front of a couple of newspaper reporters and the Cree helpers he had hired to ride shotgun in their boats, he was greasing himself up for his plunge into yet another cold waterway. He was doing it, of course, for the standard reasons – to see if he could, because nobody else had done it, because the river was there. His explanation though, could not come close to explaining his "ardent desire for distinction." Those who want to circle the globe in hot-air balloons or climb mountains are pushed by the same motivator. The slopes of Everest, fifty years after the summit was conquered by Sir Edmund Hillary, still lure those burning with the idea they have something to prove. The danger of the undertaking is a critical factor; even today, anyone going for the summit of Everest has but a one in four chance of return.

And it is predominantly a guy thing, the growing legions of stern, clench-jawed, power-suited women we encounter in the office elevator notwithstanding. Women may play at the game, but they rarely get it. It's a motion they go through without really believing in it. I can't think of one woman in whom ambition has reached disease proportions, though it has done just that in many men I know. Rather, ambition evokes in women a perplexity well-expressed by a writer in the *Guardian* newspaper: "I can only wonder," wrote Charlotte Raven in 1997, questioning the Everest climbers, "what it must be like to be the wife or girlfriend of a man who would ruin the rest of *your* life by jeopardizing his in pursuit of what? It's not as if he'd be the first. That kick I can understand, but how do you keep it special when there are queues of thrill-seekers cluttering the ascent?"

Her point underlines the difference between the arguably selfish pursuits of many so-called thrill-seekers and the more palatable intrepids of the past, like Sir Edmund, who planted flags on behalf of countrymen back home, or who believed what they were achieving was for the sake of mankind. But it also raises the little matter of what is different between women and men, not the least of which is chemical. Can women, who are governed by estrogen, not testosterone, ever hope to truly understand this matter of male wanting? And the other question we have to ask ultimately is this: does the motivation that sparks rock climbing, fighting, making money, taking over companies, writing best-sellers, chasing women, and running for office all come out of a gland?

For a century, going back to Max Weber, sociological prejudice has been against explanations that depend primarily on biology, argues Theodore D. Kemper, a St. John's University sociologist, in his book *Social Structure and Testosterone: Explorations of the Socio-Bio-Social Chain.* We all know the argument: if little boys were given dolls rather than toy guns and if violence were controlled on TV, the world would change. Boys can be nurtured away from their aggressive instincts. This notion has had currency for some twenty years, but I note that the little sons of my politically-correct-thinking friends are as raging and aggressive as boys ever were, their laser guns rat-a-tatting, their Nintendo games threatening and gory. Their parents, who thought they had it figured out, throw up their hands in bewilderment.

The back-to-biology school tells us that behind every instance of raging, aggressive ambition is a pool of testosterone, a theory given credence by the findings of a team of Georgia State University psychologists. When they measured testosterone in courtroom lawyers, they found levels that were, on average, thirty per cent higher than in the general population.

Testosterone, interestingly, doesn't work the way you might think. Contrary to the myth that surging testosterone makes a man do something, it seems that there are things you do which, as a result, induce a surge of the dreaded/wonderful hormone. Testosterone doesn't cause you to pick a fight, but it makes you feel really good after you've won it. This testosterone surge not only feels good, but it delivers results we like. "In many animal species," explains Kemper, "it is followed by increased access to sexual partners, priority access to food, and greater security from infringement on one's territory." So, like Pavlov's dogs, we will do again and again whatever we have learned will bring it on.

However, there is another fact about testosterone that is even more interesting. A surge (an elevation, to use the scientific language) can be brought on by *two* things. The first is the act of "dominance" – beating somebody up, killing something or somebody, winning a battle. But there is a second, less overtly brutal undertaking described as "anything that will achieve eminence." According to Kemper, this "involves recognition by a social group of significant personal attainment or contribution to normatively supported group goals. In this mode of social encounter, opponents do not clash, and no one is defeated. However, individually or collectively, others in the group found reason to grant approval, deference, reward, benefit, rank, and the like." His examples were of men being awarded a promotion in military rank or having a degree conferred after graduation from medical school. It could also, one might think, come from being favourably reviewed on the book page or being complimented on your tie. The important thing is that, no matter whether one's achievement is brutal or more civilized and restrained, the results are the same. "Both dominance and eminence are grounds for testosterone elevation."

If a man harnesses his ambition and uses either the urge for dominance or the urge for eminence to benefit the world and his fellows – protecting his family or community, providing leadership in the struggle to achieve a universally desired goal – it can be a wonderful thing. The problem, however, is that the urge frequently goes somewhere else. Or nowhere at all. Ambition can express itself in sundry ways. It can be social, advancing the public good, or it can be thoroughly self-indulgent. Sometimes it is both at the same time. To have it but not know what to do with it is one of the diseases of modern, post-industrial, Western man; a huge ambition to achieve accompanied by a corresponding absence of imagination or passion or care for a cause. My friend Ted did get elected and went on to land an important cabinet position. Only I (and now, of course, all of you) know the factors driving his success. Public life is so filled with men doing things for suspect or inarticulated or absent reasons, we have bountiful cause to be dismayed. Ben Pimlott, reviewing Anthony Seldon's 1997 book *John Major: A Political Life* in *The Independent*, identifies Margaret Thatcher's Conservative Party successor's great flaw as his having a huge ambition that had no overriding purpose other than its own existence. The biographer writes, "That he wanted to become Prime Minister and was one of the most ambitious men in the House of Commons, there can be no doubt." And Pimlott answers, "But ambitious for what? In the hollow unanswerability of that question lies the tragedy of Mr. Major's career." This is the tragedy of John Major's career and, we might say, the careers of too many men, including political leaders. They are ambitious, but for what?

What I notice about men in their forties, though, is an almost universal sense of urgency. We're not always sure what we should feel urgent about, but we experience the sensation. This binds us together. In our impatience we form a club. As a group, we probably get by on less sleep than any other group in society. We spout a motto: work hard, play hard. Why? Well, maybe it's because for the first time in our lives we realize our time is limited. The yellow dog of our mortality is barking at our heels. We have received the first hint that not only time, but energy and talent are truly limited. This scares the dickens out of us. It will get worse; in our fifties and sixties we will realize even more poignantly that we won't live forever, we will realize even more how limited we are. But men in their fifties and sixties also have developed a certain grace as they acknowledge this fact (maybe the result of waning testosterone). This grace has not yet been bestowed on the man in his forties; all he has is his newly discovered fear, his panic, the sense of urgency that whatever it is he wants to do or get, now is the time. He can't waste a minute.

If he is smart, a man will understand that what is required of him is the enormous task of shepherding his ambition, of understanding the whole matter of choices. By the time you are forty, as was the case for my friend Ted, the great male appetite is huge. You want sex, you want romance, you want family, you want acclaim, you want wealth, you want adventure, you want power. But it is also in the process of being tempered, mercilessly. You used to believe you could have all of the above. Now, if you are wise, you realize that there are trade-offs. And you also know that you can't afford to dither. The moment is here and fleeting fast. History may give you your quarter-hour at the podium, but then it dispassionately moves on. So much to do, so little time; the buffet table is loaded and we want some of everything, but, like the man who wins the contest to go after all the money he can grab from the bank vault, we have only five minutes in which to do it. We can hear the stopwatch ticking loudly – each tick a terror. And, like the fool in the bank vault, we risk dropping the whole bundle each time our reach exceeds our grasp. Perhaps in its way this is still Darwinian because it is a hunter-gatherer's urge, opportunistic rather than planned and methodical. Take two while you're at it because you never know if or when the chance will come again.

Months after our earlier meeting, Ted and I again meet for lunch. This time it's just the two of us. A lot has happened for him. He has an office with a spectacular view of statues and manicured lawns. He has a car at his disposal, along with a driver whenever he wants to use one. He is much in demand. His style is to call me from his car phone when he is between meetings or coming back from giving a speech at some hinterland town's chamber of commerce. He asks me to call his secretary and set up an appointment for the lunch we will have. He loves his job. Obviously he is thriving in it. He was promoted quickly, and every day delivers challenges that he relishes: problems to solve, initiatives that only he can take. He has made a kind of peace with his wife. Their Christmas card photo, which includes their three teenaged children, makes their family look like a committee.

Is he happy?

Happiness has nothing to do with it. Happiness is a term that is irrelevant. But his testosterone pumps feverishly and regularly. What's more, he knows that he learned an important lesson: you can never have everything.

Did he make the right choice? "Oh yeah." Pause. "Well, maybe."

Actually, he'll never really know.

5

Work, Money, and Toys:
The Professional ID

Where is the life in all our living? Where is the wisdom in all our knowledge?

— T.S. ELIOT

Contrary to what most people think, a workaholic is not somebody who works all the time, though routinely coming home late from the office may certainly be a symptom. A workaholic, more precisely, is somebody who only knows who he is through the work he does. His pleasure comes from his work. His role in society comes from his work. His status comes from his work. He is terrified that without his work he'd be completely adrift in all of these areas. And he's right; without the framework of work he'd be lost.

No group of people in all the world are more defined by their work than are urban Western men at midlife, primarily

North American men, but a certain class of European professional, too. The term "workaholic" was coined with us in mind. I know for a fact that I am such a workaholic. And so are Hugh and Donald. One time when I stayed in London, I got to know Hugh and Donald.

Hugh and Donald happen to be brothers-in-law who both own Saabs and live stylish urban lives. They work very hard. They are consultants. An accepted fact about their kind of work is that it keeps them travelling. During one of the weeks I was there, Donald spent the Tuesday in Dublin. He came back to London for the night with his wife and family – though he didn't see his children because his son is at boarding school and his twenty-year-old daughter has a late-night job in a restaurant – and he left the next morning for Milan. On Thursday he spent the day at his office in London, but on Friday had to fly to a meeting in Rome. The next morning, Saturday, his brother-in-law, Hugh, left at five-thirty to catch a flight to Prague.

Despite technologies and communications systems that are supposed to help keep us at home, all this travelling seemed necessary. When he was asked whether it was possible to carry on his meetings in far-flung cities via teleconference calls, Donald pointed out that you can't give people a proper dressing-down on the phone. For that you have to be there in person. Then he laughed merrily as if there were nothing in the world he enjoyed more than giving a subordinate or even a client a good bawling out. Both men accumulate extraordinary wads of air-travel reward points. One of our system's wonderful ironies is that when you fly a lot — so much that you can barely stand the sight of another departure lounge — your prize is more air travel. At a family dinner, Donald made a gift of some of his air-travel points to his mother-in-law so that she could take a winter holiday in Majorca. Everyone in the room — his family and guests — applauded the gesture, though Donald demurred. "It was nothing," he said generously. Air-travel points, however, still carry enormous cachet with the rest of us.

The week before Hugh had to go to Prague, he worked in his office in London. He left home every morning before eight o'clock and returned dog-tired each evening at about nine. One day, Wednesday, he left work early to go to his martial-arts class, which he needs to do, his wife confided, in order to reduce stress.

As is often the case with today's busy class of professionals, men in suits carrying briefcases and lap-top computers, it's hard to say exactly what either Hugh or Donald do. I know that they work long hours, travel, deal with high levels of stress, give people shit, and are paid (as Hugh lets it be known, and to which both lifestyle and possessions attest) great sums of money. But it is not like the old days where you could say reliably that the cobbler made shoes or the barber cut hair. The closest I can come to understanding it is to say vaguely that they help make systems work. An elaboration of these systems, of course, is another matter. This imprecision of function and product is a common problem among modern-day businessmen, especially consultants.

Hugh, on the face of it, tries to help a group of Czech investors get ready to set up a competing option to their country's long-distance-telephone system. In the newly free Czech market, private entrepreneurs are rushing to outflank the old state-owned systems. And these clients of Hugh's are among them. But they feel they can't do it without the assistance of consultants like Hugh who fly in and out over long periods of time from far-off places like London. One of Hugh's tasks is to set up an elaborate computer model which will tell the Czech businessmen what to expect in the cost-benefit scheme of things they are about to move into. A great deal is riding on it. The businessmen are putting their investment and their future at great risk and the business plan must cover all the bases. Whether or not the Czechs need such competition in order to have a better or cheaper phone system is entirely another matter. But the entrepreneurs who are cooking up the scheme certainly don't want to fall into a hole with it, so Hugh had better not screw up. Here's where he feels the incessant pressure. He is impelled to fret constantly over the computer model; he makes endless phone calls and sends flurries of faxes back and forth between London and Prague (exactly the kind of activity that will return the investors lots of money once they own the phone system). He needs to make sure they get all the variables in and that all the systems mesh. Some of this he can do from his office in London, but almost every week he must pack up for another trip to Prague. There, he is condemned to work lengthy hours and then, after snatching late suppers at cafés near the Charles Bridge, pass what remains of his evenings in his hotel room, while wishing rather that he were back home enjoying his garden. For this he is paid great sums of money and earns heaps of air-travel points.

Along with the matter of his ambition, that "ardent desire for distinction," the biggest problem for the midlifeman is the problem of identity. And how the work we do, and the fruits of that work, turn out to be vital to defining us, creating that identity. Again, it is a cliché and stereotypical to suggest it is not the same for women. But ask yourself how many women you know who, when asked who they are, would have as their first thought, "I am an accountant; I drive a BMW." Then think of asking the same question of men.

Donald loves his job. Few people in the world love their jobs more obviously than does Donald. He sports it like a comfortable and stylish suit. He's a partner in his company and is flattered regularly when other firms send their head-hunters to try to woo him away. They never succeed, but being pursued delights Donald and places him in a tantalizing position within his firm, envied by his peers and jealously valued by his seniors. It is great to be in demand, to be wanted. The ego glows. Donald is one of those men who seems to have had the luck or the wit to land exactly where he was supposed to in life. He enjoys his work so much – even, or perhaps especially, the meting out of scoldings – that it is no different to him than an enjoyable sport, a game he plays well and exults in. You can imagine him at the end of a sixteen-hour day of high-pressure meetings and long-distance telephone calls, towelling off, pouring a beer, and smiling broadly as he might after a good game of squash. He has lots of energy left for spending a couple of hours at the opera or watching a witty comedy show with his wife.

The more he enjoys work, the better he does at it and, like some flawlessly self-fulfilling prophesy, it compounds for Donald and his family into a great success. For him, what everyone else calls work doesn't seem like work at all. His mother-in-law (the one who got the air points for Majorca) whispers approvingly, "Donald works very hard but it doesn't matter because he loves his job and he is very good to his family." At this early moment of middle age he is on top of all his games, even the mother-in-law sweepstakes. He has the rosy-cheeked, satisfied air of a hale fellow well met. He is bright and witty, excels at the prized British sport of repartee, but seems never to descend into sarcasm or meanness. He is quick on the uptake of every pun or joke but not in a put-down mode; his is not a wit that is put to work to lance the boil of unhappiness or frustration.

Workaholics, we need to realize, have very complex relationships with a couple of other things in life. Happiness is one of them; money is the other. Should either of these ever become a problem for us, we would have a great deal of trouble sorting out our priorities and re-constituting the life we should be having.

Donald's rewards have flowed bounteously and he sports them with ease. I have no idea exactly how much money he makes from his salary, his partnership spoils, and possibly from investments and other such things. But it is easily more than enough and infinitely more than at the age of twenty or thirty he would have dreamed he had the potential – let alone the right – to make. Ever. Yet now here it is, like a faucet that has been opened for him, and he has his mouth right under the spigot.

The toys and perks are many. Donald and his wife give splashy parties in their hundred-year-old house in North London. They buy fine wine and expensive clothes and theatre tickets and trips. They take their children and their cousins and assorted friends along with them in summer and sometimes at Christmas to their converted barn in France. Their new black Saab 900, in which they zoom around London and which they take on country outings, is a ragtop, a convertible. For Donald, his career, his profession, his job has been wonderful; he would not have his identity without it. Everything that goes with it and that flows from it – the fulfillment of ambition, the toys, the money – is a lark, an extremely pleasant boat of gravy. He relishes it all.

Hugh also does well at his job. He is a manager. But, unlike Donald, he does not exult in it and never gives the impression it is anything but a worrisome, stressful chore. Hugh, unlike Donald, is not the right man in the right place. He does well because he is very bright and he is diligent, a perfectionist who won't leave even the most hated chore unfinished or uncompleted. Every detail is meticulously covered. We are having brunch at Hugh's house on a Sunday morning. The phone rings and Hugh's wife answers it. It is work, someone named

Stephen, she announces. Hugh frowns and goes to his study to take the call. Donald sniffs; he knows who has called. He ambles, holding on to his glass of orange juice and champagne, toward the French doors that look out to the garden with its bird bath and concrete statuary, not missing a beat of the anecdote he has been recounting. I ask whether he gets calls from work on a Sunday morning. He smiles. "The willing horse carries the load," he says. He is referring to Hugh, who re-enters the room now in a bad mood.

This is where the problem starts to have a nub. This is where Donald and Hugh begin to part ways. This is where the issue – for all of us – starts to get difficult (and interesting).

Deep down – or maybe not so deep down, for he is actually quite transparent about it – Hugh hates his job. Little joy or well-being springs directly from the position he holds as a professional. In fact, a simmering resentment manifests itself in a number of ways that are much more subtle than directly complaining about the job. Hugh's humour is different than Donald's; it has a sharper edge that can give way to sarcasm. His wit doesn't miss a chance to make a jab. He is a polite and a nice man, so he won't impale people who are present. But he doesn't suffer fools gladly, and is ready to flash his rapier at any system or any person he finds pontifical or pretentious or stuffy. This is the fallout from his hatred of his job; his pool of residual resentment bubbles like a geyser ready and needing regularly to blow.

What his job gives him that he wouldn't want to relinquish are his toys. Hugh and his wife (who is a scientist teaching at a college in London) are renovating their Edwardian house. Hugh likes to buy expensive antiques and also to collect art – not expensive known or current painters, but paintings he finds when he rummages around in studios or little galleries on trips to Australia or Wales. Hugh's car is also a Saab, a sport model capable of 140 miles per hour. It has chrome wheels and leather upholstery, though it is not new like Donald's. It is seven years old.

Hugh's toys are the spoils of his job and he relishes them. But he looks at them differently than the way Donald looks at his toys. Toys for Donald are like apples that fall from the tree; every time he shakes a branch they drop and remind him of his bounteous life. For Hugh, the toys are absolutely necessary as symbols and rewards; they are to be hoarded because they remind him that something must come from all his misery and all his compromises. Because he loves the toys, they are an important reason to keep on putting up with his job. He believes without his job he would not have them. But the trade-off is that he has to use them, and other means, to unwind and relieve his stress.

Hugh plays jazz piano, and another way for him to relieve stress – other than to strip paint from the stair bannisters in his Edwardian house or drive his Saab sports car really fast or hunt for paintings in little studios on the Cornwall coast or get robed in his white pyjamas and practise aikido – is to spend an hour at the keyboard improvising jazz. He is very good. He is a perfectionist. Hugh is such a perfectionist that his wife says when they are renovating the house she finds it hard to help. It is difficult for her to do things to his standard.

What Hugh really wants to do, his mother tells me in the same revealing conversation in which she has been explaining his brother-in-law Donald, is get rid of all this. She waves her hand in an expansive circle that might take in all of London. Hugh would like to chuck it all. And what would he do then? Then he would buy a manor house with some land in the country (where you can still get a very good deal, according to his mother), restore or renovate the house and gardens, and set up a retreat centre for over-stressed business-men. Men who are like he is now. There they could all indulge in aikido, gardening, renovating, painting and art appreciation classes. And Hugh would cook – "He's a very good cook," says his mother.

So why doesn't he do it?

Hugh comes back from Prague in time to have dinner with his wife and some friends who have arrived from out of town. Later, after everyone else has gone up to bed, Hugh pours a scotch. He tells me that in Prague, in his hotel room, he had been unable to sleep. It was the end of a twelve-hour day, during which he'd tried to persuade his clients to agree to his proposal for the computer model that predicted their earnings and expenses over first a three- and then a five-year term. He lay staring at the ceiling thinking that in six hours it would be morning and he would have to go back and do it all over again. His bosses at home, meanwhile, had called, pressing him about another project, overdue and stalled on his desk. "But I'm in Prague up to my ears and won't be back until Thursday, when I will still have more work to do on this one," he had protested. Well, they asked, could he come in on the weekend?

"At three a.m." he tells me, "I was lying on the floor, flat on my back, trying to summon what I knew of oriental meditation, hoping desperately to move enough of my worries out of my mind so I would be able to get to sleep. I lay there for a long time but things just seemed to get worse. I became more and more restless. Then it occurred to me that instead of simply trying to meditate my worries and problems into some buried state so that I could get to sleep, my real problem was that I had those worries in the first place. My life had got to a place where I was so overextended and so overstressed and so overburdened that at three in the morning I should have to be lying on the floor of a hotel room in Prague trying mental tricks to fall asleep."

Hugh has finally noted something his wife, his friends, his mother, even casual observers have realized for some time. But to him it came like the proverbial bolt of lightning. He knows he really needs to do something.

But what? This is Hugh's midlife crisis, if you will. It may be the most important moment of his life, one that he'll seize to make changes to his life and his direction forever. Or perhaps it's a moment he'll let pass and then regret forever.

Either way, it won't be easy. If he says yes to his moment, he'll have to embark on a huge reinvention of himself. If he says no, he'll turn into a bitter man. As we talk he tells me that lying on the floor of his hotel room he did make a decision.

"That was the moment," he says, "I decided I'd ask my superiors to go part-time. A three-day week."

I look at him. "What if they don't agree?" I ask.

"Then I'm prepared to quit," he says firmly. "My health, if not my physical health, then at least my mental health, which is probably more critical, is at stake."

In announcing his decision, Hugh suddenly looked buoyant and boyish. Despite the grey in his beard, his face beamed quite youthfully as he stood there, barefoot and in jeans, holding on to his scotch. "I'm taking control, aren't I," he said.

Perhaps. But Hugh is not out of the woods. He can't seem to stay happy for long; not even long enough to finish his drink. Reinventing oneself is the hardest thing in the world for a forty-four-year-old man, someone who has patterns and expectations, and an identity that has been built and nurtured over a long time and is deeply ingrained. If we change those things, who then are we? It's tempting to stay safely where we are, even if that means we're doomed to unhappiness.

Within minutes Hugh is struggling to justify the conclusion he has come to. He may believe he has taken control, but that responsibility is accompanied by its own brand of terror. It is strange to think that men like Hugh, these most fortunate of the fortunate, loaded with toys and comforts and opportunities, are enslaved to their good fortune. Hugh scrambles to test the plausibility of his new plan, first in terms of what he might have to give up. "This house is our biggest expense and it is almost paid off," he argues. "I drive an expensive car, but

I don't drive it very much," he goes on. "We like to ski, but that's only six times a winter. We don't eat out much. Our son is almost through university." Hugh is preparing himself for the eventuality that he will never make another penny.

Then comes a second round of rationalizations, these ones addressing the phantoms of his employers. The corporate system won't make it easy for him. That world, certainly at his level, is not kind or gentle or forgiving. Job-share notions, popular for a fleeting moment a decade or so ago, seem to have gone out the window as quickly as did car pools. "They won't let me go part-time," he says looking suddenly downcast. "They allowed one of the female consultants to go to a four-day week but it caused all sorts of administrative adjustments and they resented every one of them. It was permitted because she was a woman and she made an argument around her children and family." But Hugh's a man. "If a man asks, they take it that you are not loyal, not committed." He stops for breath. Then he goes on lamely, "I'm not ambitious to become a partner."

But he can't blame his employers or the system they represent. This is a battle he has to fight with himself. He must wrestle, like Jacob with the angel. The struggle is his alone, and so are the consequences. Hugh is in the ring, sparring through the biggest fight of his life. He now must muster all the counter-arguments. "I know I would actually do a better job, hour per hour, working part-time. I would be more rested; I could be more creative. By pursuing my other interests I would feed myself and it would show in the energy I would bring to the company's projects." He looks at me, seeking reassurance, some agreement that his argument is persuasive, that it holds water, that he isn't crazy. "I would be flexible, too. If I were sent away to Singapore on a major project I wouldn't say, 'Well, I only work three days a week.' No, I would work twelve-hour days until it was finished, I would just want to take my corresponding time off after the project was done."

Hugh's not finished yet, for now he must make the macro-argument. It would be better for the whole world if every consultant were to work part-time. "You've got ten per cent unemployment, people wasting away and doing nothing, being frustrated and having to be paid unemployment insurance and welfare and other social costs. And then you've got the rest of us working like coolies and dying from the strain. If we were to go on four day weeks and job share, we could increase the workforce in this country by twenty per cent." This, he feels, should be the coup de grâce of his argument, though he knows as well as anyone that it's not going to make much of an impression on his superiors.

Hugh drains what's left in his glass. He looks at me. I can't tell if it's a wince or a smile that he offers. "I'd better get off to bed," he says. "Tomorrow's a very early morning."

Will it be, I wonder, the first morning of the rest of his life?

6

1991

W e are on our way back to Lake of the Woods. My daughter's life has collapsed. If not collapsed, at least it has taken a good whack, the kind of buffeting a fourteen-year-old doesn't need. It is the kind of bump that, if not handled correctly in the moment, can be critical to all future life. In the last few months, her grandmother – her mother's mother – has died after a grim bout with bone cancer. Raye was a warm, lively, attractive, interesting woman who had just ended a career as a special-education teacher, only to find out within the first few months what her retirement would be: a round of doctors, hospitals, treatments, and then death. It's the first death of anyone close my daughter has ever had to deal with. But it's not all she's had to deal with; her mother has separated from her second husband and they have had to move into a smaller house. And another change: I'm no longer seeing Jane.

Sarah tries to be brave. "Well, at least we've got the cottage," she says as we speed along the Trans-Canada Highway, watching the forest of the Canadian Shield race toward and then envelop us. "That'll be something that can't change."

Playing Paul Simon worrying about being soft in the middle over and over on the tape deck – the Graceland album – we eventually get past the main glut of vacation traffic and find ourselves on the lesser-used highway that goes south from Kenora toward Sioux Narrows. This has been a wet summer; the trees look healthy and well watered. We slow for a giant snapping turtle crossing the highway – stop, get out, make sure he's safely across – then continue. All along this stretch of highway, at about five-kilometre intervals, some unknown artist has erected, atop easily visible promontories, little cairns of sharp, flat stones. They are modern yet primitive, simple and rude like the *Inukshuks* the Inuit built to guide their journeys across the treeless Arctic tundra. They seduce us back into the restful magic of this land, into a kind of mystery, unfathomable and serene, that I always think of as Ojibwa Country. Late in the afternoon we pull up the winding dirt road, the back of our car jammed with groceries and supplies. And as we coast down the little laneway toward the big house we can see, in the near distance, the glint of sun on the lake past Loon Cottage.

Rob has been working on the main house, winterizing it so that he and Barbara and their family can live more comfortably all year round. There are scaffolds up and piles of shingles, pink insulation, fresh white two-by-fours situated all around the lawn like pieces of a puzzle ready for assembly. We roll to a stop in front of the office, casting an eye to see if the Wilsons' familiar green Dodge van is parked anywhere near their cottage. Barbara emerges and greets us. Then: "I've got some bad news," she says. "Linda called a couple of weeks ago; they're not coming this year. She and Bob got divorced."

We are stunned. For my daughter this is getting worse and worse. "I'm sorry," says Barbara. "I know you guys did a lot together." She struggles to be nice but also to express her own dismay. "I'm devastated too. Personally I couldn't have been more shocked if Rob had told me he was leaving." As for us, we are thrown into a tailspin. What are we doing here? What are we going to do now? We back the car up to our door and then walk down to the rock to look out at the lake.

The first day seems kind of hopeless. Sarah wanders around in a dazed funk; not behaving badly, but looking lost. For my part, I try to be cheerful and philosophical. This alternately breaks my heart and makes me feel like an idiot. I sort deep through the memories of everything I've lost, particularly what it felt like when I was her age. In those years I had losses too: my father, three of my grandparents, and my favourite uncle. Remembering them now opens still deep wounds. I wonder if this can help me communicate some wisdom – or solace – to my daughter?

The thing is, I think I know all the right stuff: you can't hide from pain or deny it. But to instruct a fourteen-year-old to embrace it sounds way too New Age and not particularly helpful. This is the first time in years we've come on this holiday without bringing a friend along for Sarah. And with the absence now of the Wilson girls she has no one her own age to hang out with. This complicates matters in a way that is both good and bad. There is no convenient diversion for her – or for me; nothing to give us an excuse to bury and avoid all the things that look miserable and hopeless in life.

By Tuesday it looks like she is holding up pretty well. And I have an idea. We need a project. We go to the office and rent, for the rest of the week, a canoe. We pack some oranges and my Swiss Army knife. Down at the dock we strap on life vests, choose paddles that are the right size, and take the canoe, a fourteen-foot aluminum Grumman, and lift it around so we can nose it into the water. It's not the best canoe, but it's not bad. Sarah has had lots of rides in canoes, but now she will do more than ride. I'm determined that she will learn to paddle. I'll teach her whatever I know of bow work, stern work, the trusty J-stroke. How to work with a partner; how to turn the canoe end about should you happen to be alone and need to paddle it all by yourself. How to get from A to B without zig-zagging all over the lake; for, done properly, there is no greater quiet pleasure than going somewhere in a canoe.

Every day we go out. We do our lessons and get our exercise: circling the islands, cutting across the open lake against a stiff breeze. When I'm in the bow I turn around and take the quintessential photograph of my student – good grip on the paddle, lower arm straight, not bent, with a hold close to the blade – exuding real confidence in her role in the stern. There is lots of open lake to work in, but it is likewise not much of a paddle to move around the point from our cottage and cross to a dead-end bay. Here is one of the great pleasures for a canoeist. The bay is choked with water plants – lilies and rushes. It is a sanctuary for birds and turtles. At the far end is the muddy brown lump of a beaver dam. The canoe is the perfect way to drift quietly and slowly through the reeds without disturbing the life in the bay. We barely startle even the great blue heron we come upon.

Back on the open lake, we inadvertently separate a family of loons. Our arrival fails to scare them off, but with Mom on one side of us and Dad and the kids on the other, they start an incessant conversation, talking hurriedly to one another across our bow.

If I could learn any non-human language, the language I would choose would be Loon. There are at least five versions of loon talk, each differing so much from the others it's hard to believe they all come from the same bird. My field guide lists "falsetto wails, weird yodeling, maniacal quavering laughter; and at night a tremulous ha-oo-oo. In flight a barking kwuk." An early settler brought to these parts as a bride wrote about hearing the eerie calls at night and believing they were wolves. Our family converse among themselves for a minute, then it all stops for a few seconds until, on some cue spoken I'm not sure from who, they dive. We count "a thousand and one, a thousand and two, a thousand and three" until we see them reappear sixty metres away, toward the island.

7

The Annual Meeting

Bad men will be friends for the sake of pleasure or what is useful, for this is the way in which they are similar, while good men will be friends for the sake of each other, for they will be friends just because they are good. The latter, then, will be friends without qualification, while the former will be friends in virtue of some attribute and by resemblance of these.

— ARISTOTLE

For my board of directors' annual meeting this year, I decided to do what some of the big companies often do: go some place nice. We would meet overlooking a beautiful pine-shrouded lake with opportunities for swimming, fishing, and listening to the call of the loons. It made things easier that my company is just me. And my board of directors is my buddy Jake. Our place of meeting would be Jake's summer estate, which is a houseboat (actually an octagonal cedar cabin, twenty feet by twenty feet, with a vaulted cathedral ceiling, built on a platform that floats on four gigantic Styrofoam pontoons). Jake's "houseboat" is moored to an island near the fishing resort town of Minaki in the spectacular northern Ontario wilderness.

Jake is the chairman of my board of directors. He is one of my best friends, but male friendships always have to be *about* something, so we decided to make ours about work. Since we're both writers, what we call work easily spills over into the whole of our otherwise jumbled lives anyway. But guys who are self-employed need to be reminded to surround themselves with some semblance of a work ethic, so it seemed reasonable to give our connection the quasi-business label, "board of directors."

What this has meant for years is that from time to time, maybe a couple of times a month, we get together – usually over a plate of pasta at a favourite café – so I can ask him whether some action I am about to undertake, in either the professional or the personal sphere, is a good idea. Either of us can initiate a meeting. It's a mutual thing because I am also the chairman of Jake's board. Sometimes one of us will call a meeting in order to advise the other that we think he is doing something stupid. Or that we have an idea for something he might do that we think would be smart. That's what boards of directors are for, not only if you are Larry Inc. or Jake Inc., but if you happen to be the Royal Bank or Exxon or Xerox.

Jake doesn't always heed my advice. Nor do I always heed his. That's okay, there's nothing in the by-laws that says we have to follow advice. We just have to listen to it. As he says, "We don't have to paint each other's picture, but we do have to say whether or not said picture's hanging straight." Sometimes when Jake walks into a propeller, business or romantic, that I should have warned him about but didn't, I feel really bad. Sometimes he'll walk into a propeller that I did warn him about. I still feel bad. Part of the deal is that we refrain from saying, "I told you so."

Of all my friends, Jake is the one who easily has the most interesting stuff. As I wait at the top of the stairs above the boat dock in Minaki where he has agreed to pick me up, I watch him approach. He tools up in his restored 1947 Peterborough outboard. A beauty, fourteen feet of cedar and mahogany that, when I last saw it, was propped up on saw-horses in his brother-in-law's garage, where it stayed for the two winters it took to restore it. Those were long splendid evenings spent disassembling and reassembling, measuring and cutting, replacing rotted boards, lovingly sanding everything smooth. Sometimes I helped him. Sometimes others of his buddies helped him. Now the results are magnificent. The boat gleams; the hull is painted a deep red; the gunwales and upper deck have been varnished with so many coats bullets could be deflected.

"We have to wait for Ritchie," says Jake as he steps out and walks up the dock that basks in August sunshine. I wasn't expecting this. Ritchie is another guy we've both known for years; he edits a magazine we've both worked for on occasion. I pause for a moment to let the new information sink in; Ritchie's presence will change the dynamic. But that's okay, I decide quickly. It won't affect the meeting. We'll designate him a consultant to the process.

The nature of male friendship is easy to fathom so long as you keep one very simple matter in mind: the abiding mythology of male friendships is that everything is always about something else, a project or an activity. Men are friends with the guys they play poker with, the guys they go hunting with, the men they work with, the men they play baseball with. No male friendship is ever only about friendship. (This is how men through history have simultaneously been able to get things done – you could plan and wage a war or a political campaign, build a television network or an airline, or engineer a flight to the moon, all while enjoying your male association.) Material stuff is a great basis for a friendship. The men who sit in coffee shops on rainy days talking about pressure pumps and winches or getting an air-conditioning system to work are in the midst of enjoying highly satisfying friendships. These are also useful friendships because the interchange is a way of solving problems. Like the human or romantic relationships that women seem to discuss endlessly in their friendships, such things as engines and pressure pumps and cooling systems are constantly giving problems. They can always stand improvement. You never tire of talking about them around the table because somebody will always have an idea. There is the off-chance it could even be a good idea.

The other thing about male friendships is that no friendship is exclusive. Which is a very important way to understand the difference between attachments men have to other men and the attachments we have to women. Jealousy is not a feeling men keep close at hand – if it is entertained at all in our thoughts – about the loyalty or enjoyment of other men. Nor does there even seem to be the sort of hierarchy leading to the position of "best friend" that I deem to be a factor of such paramount importance in, for instance, my daughter's relations with her female associates. Which is why it's okay that Ritchie shows up to join us on this particular day. The friends you go fishing with do not get jealous of the friends you play ball with or those with whom you have an investment club. There is room for both. There is perhaps not even any overlap.

Ritchie arrives, and we speed away from the Minaki town dock, waving as we roar past the holiday lodge; three middle-aged men in an antique boat. In about ten minutes we've arrived at the houseboat in its blissfully quiet, secluded cove. It's just after noon; time for a swim and a beer and a gander through the binoculars at a family of mallards and a doe that can be seen carefully edging through the trees toward the water, half a mile down the shore. After a couple of hours of this we agree it's time to head across to a different quiet bay to do some casting. When Jake was younger, in his twenties, he made extra money as a guide, taking businessmen or retired cops from Chicago out fishing. So he knows the spots where a walleye ought to be waiting in the reeds.

We cast for a bit, and it occurs to me what a wonderful role fishing plays in the life of my friend Jake. It is a constant, and one that keeps everything else in a marvellously balanced perspective. Day in, day out, year after year, fishing doesn't change. Whatever else might come and go, jobs and loves and riches and fame, fishing is a steadier. But after a bit, I also notice that the conversation has somehow turned. This now isn't about fishing; this is the meeting. It's time for each of us to give an accounting of himself and absorb the feedback. Ritchie has been telling about some woman he's chasing but now he's quiet. Listening. Each of us is here with his private agenda, with his list that includes thinly veiled hurts and worries and uncertainties. There are successes too; we need to report some triumphs.

"Self," someone once said, is actually "others." Or at least, self would not exist without others; self-consciousness comes from response to others and from the response of others to you. Jake breaks the ice. He's starting a new novel and complains he's not having an easy time of it. He has to make decisions, for example, about the voice he might use and which of several possible characters to select as his main one. The problems we start to bat about are our frustrations with our work, like the men who can't get the air conditioning to function. Yet, though we presume this is only about work, our association leaves the door wide open to accommodate everything else, whether it's a marriage coming undone or how we're doing with our children. By nurturing the illusion that we care mainly about our work, we somehow take the fearful edge off these other topics. Jake turns abruptly and asks if I'm making any money. The urge to embellish – even to lie – is always there; men don't like to tell one another that things are going badly. But Jake and I can see through one another's bull-shit. Besides, here's where our model is important: the first rule of business is that you don't lie to your board of directors.

Jake claims it was I who first gave him the courage to be a writer, a flattery I enjoy, though I might say he did the same for me. When we met, in our mid-twenties, if I possessed anything, it was simply a kind of foolhardy bravado that made me believe I could avoid having to get a real job if I doggedly peddled my story ideas and articles around to magazines. There were a handful of us – Jake and I and a couple of other friends, Charles and John – all in the same boat. Perhaps our greatest immediate accomplishment is that all four of us have been able to lead reasonably productive lives for twenty-five years while consistently cheating the nine-to-five routine. Now, in middle age, we can assume certain things about our professions. It was our friendships, though, that both gave strength and brought authenticity to the adventure. We had no mentors; we were entirely on our own. And somehow we unwittingly gave one another courage. Without one another, we would have been will-o'-the-wisps. Together, we became a community. We didn't define one another necessarily, but we forced each other, whenever necessary, to define himself.

The worst moments were when jealousies entered. Or flashes of envy. We kept track of each other's productivity. How many books has he got? How many films has he worked on? How much money has he made? Self-doubts and insecurities were still the demons. If one of the others was having a huge success, you could be thrilled for him and wish him well, knowing that your advice had been part of getting him there. But it was then important for turns to be taken. Elementary playground etiquette. Though I tried my best not to let it show, if any of the others had two successes in a period when I had none, it bothered me. Three successes during a period of drought for any of the rest of us would have done damage to the friendship. A kind of lock-step equality was important.

When I had a success, I was careful not to gloat. I was conscious about pulling back and hoping nothing new would come along before one of the others had a turn. It was important not to get too far ahead, just like when, in the third grade, I faked a difficulty in reading so that I could stay close to (and in solidarity with) my good friend George, who was having a genuine difficulty with reading.

A slight could be felt deeply. A certain kind of comment or even a certain kind of advice could be interpreted as a betrayal. One time, one of the friends made a "why bother" comment about a project that I was hopelessly overextended on, yet determined to see through to some completion. This was not what I needed from him. I was annoyed. The comment got my back up and put me off the friendship for a couple of months. It affected my trust and hardened my attitude. He became, for a while, not a trusted friend but a goad. I would persevere despite him. Success would be my vindication.

Jake never did that. He saw immediately the need to persevere in everything. He also understood the nuts and bolts of practicality. Of all my friends, Jake was the one who most consistently interjected a pragmatic note. He would ask the hard questions about your game plan or your business plan; he wanted to hear not about your ambition, but about your strategy. You could be a writer or a documentary maker, but you couldn't do it on air, and Jake made you remember this. "Where's the money going to come for this one?" he would ask.

When we get around to this part of the discussion today he has advice: "You'd be doing a lot better if you were making more cold calls. You should be out knocking on a lot more doors, not just waiting for the jobs to come to you." Ritchie chimes in about some guy who came by his office the week before to try to pitch him something and how he told him to get lost. The story of his refusal turns out to be a lesson in approach. Ritchie is our litmus test; if we learn what doesn't work with him, we can make a judgement about what might work with the people we want to impress. Or what might not work.

Night falls, and at about ten o'clock the moon rises. Like a giant blood orange sneaking up over the spruce- and pine-forest horizon. We've demolished a big part of a leg of lamb done on the barbecue that serves as Jake's stove. Ritchie has brought out cigars. "Flor Extra Fina" from Cuba, "Tabaccos Esquisitos" advertise the labels. I tell him that the last time I smoked a cigar I would have gladly sold my mouth the next morning, would anyone have agreed to take it. Ritchie laughs. "These are good cigars," he says. And he is right. He strips off his shorts and cannonballs bare-ass into the moonlit water, all the while yakking about how he hopes a big muskie fish won't swim up from underneath and bite him. You can't parody guy stuff; it's too much right there in front of you. Simple and unselfconscious. Ritchie gets out of the water and dries himself off. Jake says, "Okay boys, get in the boat, it's time for our moonlight cruise." He steps in and fires up the thirty-horsepower Yamaha.

In the back of the boat he has stuck his guitar. It's the kind of experience you dream about having with every pretty woman you've ever known, and here I am having it with Jake and Ritchie. We speed under the winsome light to the middle of the lake, the place we were earlier when we believed we might get some walleye to bite. Among the shadows along the south shore, we can see the gleaming boathouses of the summer people. Jake cuts the engine and we bob for a long minute in the sweet nighttime silence. He hands the guitar to Ritchie. Time to sing. Three guys, average age approaching fifty, and we're going to serenade each other in the middle of a Canadian lake on a hot August night. Ritchie, who's got a surprisingly melodious voice, gives up a Gordon Lightfoot ballad from about 1967. He hands the guitar to Jake who is, by far, the most accomplished strummer among us. Johnny Rivers's "I Washed My Hands in the Muddy Water." Then it's my turn. "Do something religious," says Jake. Something from out of that Baptist rural past. Jake grew up Catholic, a religion that, whatever its considerable strengths and accomplishments, has produced little music that can be accompanied by a six-string acoustic guitar. I accept the instrument. It's been a few years since I've held a guitar and even then I could only master about three chords, maybe five if I counted a couple of minors. I strum for a few seconds, trying to remember how the fingering goes. I think back, attempting to recall a repertoire. Then I have an idea. "Just a closer walk with thee . . ." The perfect song for a group of friends. For guys. "Let it be, dear Lord, let it be."

8

Love Forty: What I Learned from Tennis

Life is a game. Some play it well, others don't.

— FROM THE 1993 CHINESE MOVIE
Life on a String

My first (and only) tennis instructor was a tall, blonde Californian who, even though she lived in Toronto, where she taught at Glendon College, never lost the tiniest degree of her golden, California tan; it was as if she'd been dyed in it. She had a languid, lazy, American way of talking that we inhibited, winterized northerners found as sexy as syrup. You were lulled as you listened, and after a while lost conscious awareness of even hearing anything. She was probably about twenty-four, not much older than her gawky, pimple-faced, trying-so-very-hard-to-be-worldly students. Yet those few years made all the difference. Those few years, combined with her size – she was over six feet tall, perfectly proportioned, and gorgeous. The cumulative effect inspired awe; the only possible response was to gasp and grow silently submissive in her presence. It was as if we had encountered a cloud bank, an entire warm front from the Pacific.

We paid attention to our tennis. I remember vividly the separate lessons. Serve. Return. Go to the net. For some reason I missed the session on backhand and, consequently, my backhand remained weak and less than effective for most of the years since. But I think about our instructor frequently when I'm playing tennis. I never take hold of a racquet without a flicker of memory bringing into focus someone blonde and Californian making sure I don't forget the fundamentals of my grip.

I think about tennis more than I play it. It provides endless things to think about, especially these days of my developing middle age. The championship tournaments are played by young people, most of them barely out of, if not still in, their teens. Boris Becker was seventeen when he won his first grand-slam event. The women are even younger; Martina Hingis was fifteen. But I like to think of tennis as a middle-aged thing, a sport for forty-year-olds. Tennis, in fact, could be a metaphor for all that confronts and confounds the midlifeman. It could be, likewise, a metaphor for all the responses required of us.

What is important in playing tennis is likewise important in life, but it took me until I was in my forties to understand this. For instance, when do you go to the net? This is an important instinct in tennis, and not one bit less so in life. In tennis the right mix of serve and volley can be the key to your game. Your abrupt appearance in front of your opponent, after your rush to the net, is bound surely to keep him off guard and off speed. He looks up, and there's your nose and the whites of your eyes. You are placed perfectly to demolish him, before he can get into position, with a drop shot or a solid smash. Going to the net is smart and agile and full of calculation and instinct and bravado. But if your timing is bad, it can also fail miserably.

The potential to fail is elemental to the risk. It's interesting to watch even Sampras or Agassi standing flat-footed at the net while their opponent lobs an over-the-head that they can't run backwards quickly enough to retrieve. But the breathless beauty and triumph of a good forehand volley also comes out of the risk. Nothing in tennis or in life seems really much of an achievement if the chance in going for it hasn't offered at least an equal possibility for failure.

In going to the net, though, it seems to me the real risk is in our hesitation. If we hesitate, we fall into a clumsiness of timing that gets us into position too late. Or too early. Or only halfway there. No one who hesitates is more lost than the tennis player who hesitates in going to the net. So what we confront within ourselves when we face the issue of going to the net is the whole matter of our indecisiveness. And the whole matter of our being able (or not able) to size up a moment and seize its opportunity. The responsibility resting on our slim shoulders is so huge and so private and so existential, one feels Kierkegaard would be impressed.

Then there is the serve. No one is asked to be Richard Krajicek or Greg Rusedski, delivering at an overpowering 120 m.p.h. But our serve *is* the way we address the world. Do we serve with power, or with trickery? Are our serves predictable, landing always in the same place, or will our opponent be a little unsure as to where they will show up? Do *we* know where they'll show up? The serve is both our calling card, and it's what puts us in the game. It's what others have no choice but to respond to. It deserves our endless work.

A very telling question, whose answer reveals a lot about our character, is this: what do we do after faulting on a first serve? For the fault is a failure, if ever so small, and what's critically important in tennis, as in life, is not what we do after success, but after failure. Specifically, what do we do when the rules or luck or life itself generously gives us a second chance? One of the wonderful rules of tennis is that built-in second chance after a first delivery that has gone too wide or too far or not far enough. But the opportunity brings us to our problem: are we able to treat this second chance as a fresh opportunity, mindless of our initial error? Do we learn from our first mistake and alter our approach on this second chance? Are we gamblers, going for broke, not caring that our percentage chance has been cut in half? Or has our failure rendered us dispirited and timid; does our second serve become a safe lob, arriving like a pizza delivery, with no more than half the velocity and intensity of the first try?

How does our opponent think of us in this regard; does he know what to expect? I play with a partner who sizzles his first service, always placing it close to one or another of the lines, and requiring me to run and reach. But whenever he misses on that first serve I can depend one hundred per cent on his lobbing an easy one right into the centre of the service court. He is totally consistent in this; his predictability is my private joke on him. He's so afraid of double faulting at that moment, he ignores all other aspects of his game strategy and invariably delivers something I can easily put away for the point. I'm always ready for him, so what good has it done him? The fact that this is his pattern of play I take not just as a tennis decision, but a character trait, one so deeply ingrained in his psyche and mode of behaviour that he doubtless never thinks of it consciously.

Lastly, the most important and revealing moment of all in one's tennis game is that time when you find yourself down. Behind in the score by a little. Or a lot. Tennis, to paraphrase what Yogi Berra said so perfectly of baseball, is never over until it's over. It has the blessing of not being ended arbitrarily by the clock or even the finish line. This means you can be down two sets to zero, five games to nil, defending at forty-love, and in theory still come back to win the match. You always have a chance for the comeback. But you cannot do it – not ever – without a certain strength of mind and character, a steeliness of will, a reserve tank of determination, an iciness of fortitude that doesn't give in so long as there are any odds left in your favour. It all has to do with what is wonderfully termed "digging deep."

The ability to dig deep is doubtless one of the most

important attributes we can ever have in life. And it's important to get it by now; after forty we're going to need it a lot.

One thing I note, now that I play tennis with a set who are aging, slipping increasingly deeper into middle age, is the number of our infirmities that need to be dealt with. I feel like a veritable healthy child compared to some of these players. They have knee braces to strap on, back supports to put in place, special orthopedic shoes to wear. But play they do. Not long ago I had a doubles match against a fellow who was three weeks away from hip-replacement surgery. He was indomitable. He and his partner had figured out that she would have to do the running, but in the meantime he had perfected a repertoire of trick and top-spin shots that, particularly when delivered from the vicinity of the fault line, put me and my partner away almost every time. David had learned to compensate for his lack of mobility. His smarts had surpassed and replaced his brute strength. There are still too many of us who haven't learned this. There are still a lot of forty-five-year-old illusions walking around, just back from twenty-thousand dollar tennis camps in Florida where they were led to believe they might still take on Pete Sampras. But they'll have to learn it. And when they do, I believe they'll be not only better tennis players, they'll be more fully realized human beings.

9

The Face I Deserve

Man has no body distinct from his soul, for what is called body is that portion of the soul discerned by the five senses. . . . Energy is the only life and is from the body, and Reason is the bound or outward circumference of energy.

— WILLIAM BLAKE

A man, by the time he is forty, will have the face he deserves. When this observation was made to me just after I had passed my fortieth birthday, I found it amusing. Now I consider it every time I look at myself in a mirror. If true, you could say this is the most superb piece of natural justice next to death itself. Think about it when you next look at the mug shots in the business sections of important newspapers.

The theory, though, is sobering news. What kind of face do we have? If it is the face we deserve, is it also then the face we have earned – each line or wrinkle a testament to the story? Indeed it is. There is no fooling; the sly, arrogant, ugly, stupid, or slippery spirit must show as readily as the spirit that is generous or wise.

The operative word is "deserve," for the face you get is not necessarily the face you want, or the face you might try to fashion – or buy – through tanning spas, cosmetics, or even a good barber. Someone remarked of Oscar Wilde as he approached the moment of his celebrated trial – fat, loose, heavy-jowelled from indulging his famously uncontrolled appetites – "all his bad qualities began to show in his face."

Our face is our calling card. It is a compendium of our genetic heritage, our personal history, and our individual character. When I look at mine in the mirror I see flashing reminders of my parents and my grandparents thirty or forty or fifty years ago, the way they looked in family photographs. I might also foresee a semblance, twenty-five years from now, of the face of my child. Or even my grandchildren, yet unborn. Then I note other things, things that have to do with my very individual history. I can easily find faint evidence, still traversing the bridge of my nose, of the smash of another player's hockey stick when I was eighteen. I examine the depth and trajectory of creases lining my brow and crow-footing the corners of my mouth and eyes, and try to think, for example, how worry lines created by being independently employed differ from those I might have earned had I knuckled under a boss for twenty-five years. I look for the evidence that I might have spent too much (or not enough) time in the sun or the wind. For evidence that I have laughed, been happy, loved.

For decades our faces have been sufficient for passports and drivers' licences. Businesses and the security industry claim they soon will have refined biometrics to the point where they will be able to use the distinct individuality of our face in a digitized version as a sort of physical passport, guaranteed failsafe in permitting (or restricting) access to everything from bank machines and workplace computers to the fitness club. Technologies currently under development will combine things called "eigenfaces" with local feature analysis to make the image of our face, indisputably individual, the key to security devices.

Our life is in our face. This should not preclude care, though, in making quick judgements of others. Charles Darwin feared his face might keep him from sailing on the *Beagle*. The captain, Darwin wrote, "doubted whether anyone with my nose could possess sufficient energy and determination for the voyage." There would have been little hopeful to offer him on that score; through all of life, apparently, our noses and our chins continue to grow. The captain, however, by holding a prejudice in check, allowed Darwin to change the world.

Some men are not content with the face that time, nature, and genetics has given them, and venture further than the tanning spa to try to alter it. Cosmetic surgery, formerly almost the exclusive preserve of wealthy women, now attracts more and more men. A dermatologist I know tells me that middle-aged men, men between the ages of forty-five and sixty, are his fastest-growing new clientele. The procedures they want include having their ears pinned back, having excess skin and fat removed from the upper eyelids, having fat from the abdomen transferred to the cheeks and chin, and liposuction, which is a dastardly-sounding procedure that involves liquefying fat and then sucking it away. Men who want to have their bodies or their faces sculpted through such procedures are willing to fork out anything from $3,000 to $20,000.

This is a vanity we're not completely comfortable with as yet on a cultural level. When one poor chap in Toronto wrote about his chin tuck in an article in the *Globe and Mail*, letters poured in, howling with derision. Still, he did it. As did more than 99,000 men in the United States in 1998.

Why? Is there an emerging aesthetic of the male face that hasn't existed before? Perhaps it's okay if that's the case; all matters of taste are subjective, and the aesthetics of the face should be no less so. But what are almost a hundred thousand middle-aged American (and we don't know how many Canadian) men really doing, and why? What or who are they attempting to cheat? Does it work?

These men, by and large (as with women who go for cosmetic surgery), seem to be seeking not so much to change their faces as to keep them. They have decided to attempt to halt or disguise as many of the visible signs of aging as possible. They are hoping to stop the clock.

Ah, the clock. Linear time is a human construct, tyrannical in its relentless ticking, its harsh measurement, its apportionment of seconds, minutes, days, months, decades, millennia. We might rebel. We might wish for something more elastic. We might want a pause button such as we have on our VCR. Yet time and opportunity march on.

But though linear time is a human construct, aging is a biological fact. Despite our protests and our misgiving, biological passage carries its own irrefutable rationale, an intrinsic wisdom. Nature is full of predictable, periodic changes: summer arrives, followed by autumn. The leaves change colour. There is no reason the arrival of the deserved face should not also be one of nature's ordained gifts.

"Personality," postulated Carl Jung, "is the supreme realization of the innate idiosyncrasy of a living being. It is an act of high courage flung in the face of life, the absolute affirmation of all that constitutes the individual, the most successful adaptation of the universal conditions of existence coupled with the greatest possible freedom for self-determination. To educate a man to this seems to me no light matter."

It is the job of life to build the qualities of our character. And while he might be cut a bit of slack when younger, by the time a man is in his forties, such character as he is going to have ought to be revealed. If we don't possess any desirable qualities by this time, it will mean we haven't been doing our life work. And if we don't show anything we're proud of, it is likewise too late; it will mean we're doomed never to possess

the critical cogs, the strength of mind and character, the apti-
tude to either take hold of or wait out the game when it
might be going against us. Our forties are when we must have
achieved the character qualities that define us and with which
we will continue to live. And our face will reveal them, no
matter what.

It is as if nature uses this moment to mark us; we have
been given four decades of carte blanche, of tabula rasa, to try
to get it right – which is a pretty generous allotment when
you think about it. And now the label is finally going to be
whacked onto the forehead like a price sticker at the supermarket; there is no hiding or disguising who you are.
Everybody will know your value and will be able to know it
readily, simply by looking at you.

10

I'm about to do something that I'll feel bad about for a week. I am going to spend days riven by guilt as I try to make up and put things right. But right now I don't care. I'm going to ask some people to shut off their music. Not people like the idiots on my street in the city who play rap or Metallica at five zillion decibels late at night. The invention of electricity and then of amplified speakers once and for all changed notions of urban privacy and intrusion, and it doesn't make me feel guilty to fight back. But no, I'm going to ask some older retired people, the couple who have taken over the Wilson cottage next door, not to play Mantovani on their deck to celebrate Sunset.

I try to explain my impending action to my daughter.

"We have to nip this in the bud," I say. "Otherwise it'll be every night and we'll never be able to hear the loons."

"Try not to be too rude," she counsels.

I try.

I've been working on too many things. I am, as they say, "stressed out." I generally love working, so stress isn't something that troubles me a great deal. I fear boredom infinitely more than overwork. Yet I have a notion of my limits, and they have been exceeded. I've let it happen and I know it. I need the antidote. So for weeks I've been dreaming of this fifteen-day interlude when I will sleep early and I will sleep late. I may sleep in the middle of the afternoon. I'll read, or just stare at the water. I'll go for long swims. I'll experience the delicious sensation of tension receding, ebbing away as if through a drain in the floor, and leaving me empty and refreshed.

After I get caught up on my work and my sleep and my sanity, I'm going on an adventure. To Africa. This won't be my first trip; two years ago I had the opportunity to hire an African crew and shoot footage in then (and still) civil-war-torn Angola for a North American television documentary. It was one of the toughest trips of my life. But I caught the bug, you might say. Actually it wasn't a difficult bug to catch; Africa has long lived in my imagination. When she was a young woman, one of my grandmothers had worked for the Livingstone family, relatives of the famous doctor. So as I was growing up, stories of Dr. Livingstone and fantasies of the fabled continent infected our family and our house. I would go to sleep at night and dream of Victoria Falls.

When I decided that this could be the year to return to Africa, I invited a photographer friend to consider making the trip with me. Cheryl and I had worked together already and decided we wanted to again. Here we could work as a team — I'd write and she could take the photographs. We'd find magazines and publishers to pay for the expedition by giving us assignments in Kenya and Zimbabwe. In order to make plans, Cheryl would have to come for a few days to Loon Cottage.

After a week with me, Sarah left to go for a stint at the YMCA camp up the lake. Cheryl blew in with her swimming flippers and her notebooks. We cooked dinners combining three cheeses with our pasta sauce and drank lots of red wine. We went for long canoe rides, searching among the islands for the home nest of the eagles we could see hunting every afternoon in front of the cottage. And every morning we spread out our maps and notepads to plan our winter in Africa. We thought about itineraries; we laboured over budgets. I gave her Edward Rice's *Captain Sir Richard Frances Burton* to read, a recounting of the adventure and disaster-loaded 1857 trip with John Hanning Speke, inland from Zanzibar in search of the headwaters of the Nile.

The Mantovani couple left to go back to the city. Feeling a bit sheepish, I'd had them over for drinks one afternoon. I felt an urge to apologize but stifled it because I still felt that I'd done what I had to do. Yet I didn't want them to think badly of me; I didn't want them to leave with a one-dimensional picture of the Mantovani Killer. A drink, I felt, was the neighbourly thing; it would shore me up a bit with them, as well as ease my conscience. It was hard to tell where I stood. They eyed me the way the natives must have looked at missionaries who came to forbid their pagan practices. I couldn't have blamed them had they been resentfully busy plotting some sort of revenge.

One afternoon I left Cheryl and went by myself to the Indian reservation at Onigaming to see Norman Copenace. It had now been three years since my book *Indian Country* had been published. One of the pleasures of writing and documentary-making is the excuse each enterprise provides to move into other worlds, other people's worlds. Sometimes I know I'm an intruder. Other times I'm surprised and over-whelmed by the hospitality and the welcome that gets extended; the people I meet, some of whom become friends, I'd never have a chance to meet otherwise. Such a life is a perfect fit for someone like me who thinks of himself as the perpetual visitor.

When I did research for *Indian Country*, the Ojibwa (who are relatives of the Chippewa tribes in the U.S.) of Onigaming were one of the subject communities. And Norman was then their chief. Many pleasant autumn after-noons were spent in his company while he pulled medita-tively on an Export A cigarette and explained everything from the harvesting and curing procedures for wild rice, to the story of how his people got the Canadian government to build them a school. My fondest hope about going to do some work in Africa, I realized, was that similar opportunities would present themselves there; I might meet the tribal equivalent somewhere in Shonaland of Norman Copenace.

On a sunny afternoon I set off for Onigaming. Out on the highway I realize once more how impossible it is to understand this country without being overwhelmingly aware of the Indians. We of European stock are, after all these centuries, still somehow out of place. Like perpetual tourists. Sioux Narrows is the name both of a summer resort town and a steep, rocky channel separating the south shore of Long Point Island from the mainland. Now it's a tourist town. But it was always a place that drew people with souvenir hunting – if not outright mischief – on their minds. For a few decades a couple of hundred years ago, the Sioux would come every summer in raiding parties from the south, intent on pillaging what they could from the Ojibwa encampments. They raided all along these shores for another hundred miles to a place called Sioux Lookout. Eventually fed up, the Ojibwa held a council and decided to retaliate. They selected Sioux Narrows as the strategic spot for their battle. When a party of Sioux were sighted a day's paddle away in Whitefish Bay, the Ojibwa prepared. Warriors concealed themselves among the rocks and bushes at the top of the narrows, where they waited for the marauders' canoes to pass beneath them. When they did, arrows and rocks were let loose. As the canoes sank, the interloping braves left flailing in the water were attacked with tomahawks and knives until no Sioux was left alive.

Today, a wooden span bridge reaches across the narrows, and on both sides of the historic location, the Indians have been turned into cartoon chiefs and braves, tomahawks aloft, on gigantic signs advertising tourist gift shops. The parking lots are lined with cars and motor homes bearing plates from Illinois, Iowa, and Arkansas, present-day marauders from the south. The real Indians are not so readily visible. Though you can sometimes encounter them late in the afternoon when they have to come in to the store for gas or groceries, they remain, for the most part, hidden off in the bush, on the islands, and in the little patchwork of government-issue plywood bungalows gathered like a nest of mallard eggs behind the band office, the social-services building, and the ragged baseball diamond of Onigaming.

When I turn off the highway at Onigaming I ask a woman walking on the road where I might find Norman. The stress that rendered me so edgy a week ago seems now, in the hazy gold of afternoon in this place with its dusty road and sparkling water, and dogs lying asleep, somehow absurd. Ridiculous. A couple of kids rattle by on busted-up bicycles. The woman points to a knot of newer houses a little higher on the hill above the lake. A kind of subdivision. Norman is no longer chief, he was deposed in an election the year after I wrote my book. I don't know quite what he does now; a little of this, a little of that. For a while he had a job on the tribal education authority. He fishes in the summer and hunts in the fall and goes with his wife on long car trips to visit her relatives near Lake Superior. I drive slowly up the road. Then I spot him, a lanky, stooped man in a blue-and-purple checkered shirt, throwing horseshoes alone in his yard.

11

Life with Hugh Hefner

---

*Desire for me was always the fulfillment of a fantasy –
not a surprise or a shock, but something studied in
advance, dreamed and premeditated. It was pleasure
prepared, the completion of a thought begun in a vision.
Desire was familiar and fixed, not something new but an
older, deeper wish with a history, an embrace that had
already shadowed forth in my mind. It was something
specific, like a gift I yearned for.*

– PAUL THEROUX, The Lepers of Moyo

Playboy has made one very substantial contribution
to North America's sexual culture. Not so much by bringing
nudity into the mainstream or turning sex into play, though
the magazine and its founding editor, Hugh Hefner, cam-
paigned tirelessly and, to a degree, successfully, to do those
things. But the magazine's real revolutionary impact came

from something not quite so expected, and that was the introduction into our realm of possibilities the combination of variety and regularity. When it came to the matter of attractive women, young men learned to believe there was no need to be content with just one, another would be along in a month. There were endless possibilities; the well would never run dry.

I try to imagine my life without Hugh Hefner, and it is difficult to do so. I purchased my first *Playboy* when I was thirteen. Under severe dread of being caught or found out, I took it home under my coat and kept it hidden in the predictable place – beneath my mattress. From there it was handily available whenever I desired, shall we say, education. The models were typical examples of their era: overly ample chests, beehive hairdos, a standard of beauty that switched back and forth between Jayne Mansfield and Sandra Dee. The presentation was likewise delicately restrained by the prevailing social code; all of the models were positioned in discreet turned-away or leg-across poses. Any scientifically minded adolescents who wanted to learn something reliable about anatomy would have to wait a few years, until Hefner's more raunchy competitors and imitators pushed the envelope, forcing him to play gynecologically explicit catch-up.

But *Playboy* did the job; for us this was sex. Our doorway to the mysteries. As Camille Paglia has pointed out, pornography is male, conceptualizations repeatedly renewed. "Women have conceptualized less in history not because men have kept them from doing so, but because women do not need to conceptualize in order to exist" (*Sexual Personae*, 1990). As men, we needed to know we existed, so we conceptualized like crazy. And over the years I continued to look at the magazine, always carefully of course; one never loses a habit or a manner of behaving, particularly a furtive one. Even after the magazine made it onto the main sections of the newsstand racks I imagined my mother or my grade-school teacher might be standing there when I turned around. And then where would I be?

We could tell that Hefner put a lot of energy into trying to impose a veneer of intellectual and cultural respectability over a basically tits-and-ass venture. He seemed to want the magazine's huge commercial success to look like it came from ideas rather than prurience. Maybe he figured his audience wanted this too, in case they needed help rationalizing their purchase. So *Playboy* championed liberal causes in its editorials, from freedom of speech to marijuana decriminalization, and took on what was viewed as the tight-ass hypocrisy of mid-century Middle America's sexual views. This was okay; it was fun to know a fight was being mounted. Hypocrisy makes for a great target; it barely moves so attacking it is like shooting dairy cows. But the ploy was a diversion. Though we magazine buyers may have supported the editorials, we never lost sight of the fact that it was the pictures for which we shelled out money. It wasn't the *Atlantic Monthly*, it was a masturbatory aid. So it's not surprising the magazine never gelled as a culturally significant item by fighting for liberal causes. In fact, it seemed it was totally outflanked in its hopes for a weighty (if irreverent) respectability; as soon as the sexual revolution helped North America escape from the prudery that made it difficult to own up to buying and looking at a magazine like *Playboy*, feminism came along and rendered it politically incorrect to do so. Hugh Hefner appeared bewildered. It was as if he realized he would never be acknowledged as the intellectual heavyweight or social revolutionary he fancied he was. He wanted credit for fomenting the sexual revolution; he wanted credit for changing popular conceptions of beauty and altering the place of women in society. Nobody was going to give him that credit. And when Bob Dylan and the Rolling Stones emerged as role models for the sixties generation, their style made Hefner look anachronistic indeed.

I never pretended that I bought the magazine to read the articles. It wasn't about words. The pictures were the thing. The picture as icon has had a long history in Western culture and religion, but our century is the first to know the bonding, community-making power of mass distributed, shared images. *Playboy*'s visuals were generously shared. And the careful attention to the details of the lives of everybody who showed up in the magazine, from Hefner to the article writers and the photographers – including silly little things like the models' home towns, and their pet peeves – after a while created a sort of virtual community. In some (possibly pathetically twisted) way, the women on *Playboy*'s pages became my friends – the sort of friendships small children have with made-up characters. I can picture and put names to a number of these girls from memory. I followed some of their careers, like that of

Patti McGuire, who married the tennis player, Jimmy Connors; or their tragedies, like the one that befell the lovely blonde Playmate of the Year, Dorothy Stratten, who was murdered by her jealous husband. I waited impatiently to see some of my favourites again, hoping they would be granted repeat pictorials. I'd still like to see how Brittany York, an English woman who could speak four languages, including Mandarin Chinese, has turned out. It was particularly interesting (in the salacious way something can be arousing and embarrassing at the same time, or can be arousing by being tawdry) to watch the ones we were made to know Hefner was sleeping with – Barbi Benton, Sondra Theodore, Shannon Tweed, and of course Kimberley Conrad, whom he eventually married.

The magazine, and Hefner himself, claimed to offer that most powerful tool for an imagination, the possibility of an "alternative lifestyle." Remember, we were teenagers living with our parents, so this had wild appeal. It gave us a standard for how the cool and worldly man behaved; which cars to drive, drinks to mix, clothes to wear, opinions to hold. For me, the wannabe writer, some of the most powerful images were the portraits of the magazine's contributors on the Playbill page. When I look at them now they appear a bit wizened, but in the formative years of my youth these characters set a kind of model: hip, sagacious guys with touches of grey at the temples or in the beard. To be a photographer who shot centrefolds was fantasy beyond reach. But it seemed possible that diligent attention to one's writerly or illustrational craft might eventually get you up there, sharing space with the likes of John Updike or Shel Silverstein. What parties those guys must have been able to casually walk into — past the rest of us, our noses pushed up against the glass.

Yet there was, at the same time, something a bit sad about it all — and therefore troubling. Something that, even though we couldn't resist it, we all knew was juvenile and arrested. Gay Talese described Hefner as promoting "health through hedonism." But the last thing Hefner looked, in all the pictures we saw of him, was healthy. As the model of physical and sexual virility shifted to emphasize toned fitness, Hefner remained pale and skinny; the copious quantities of Pepsi he consumed must have kept him on a constant caffeine high. He smoked a pipe, which looked silly both on him and on any young man who tried to emulate him. Which is probably why so few did, and pipe-smoking among the young and the hip never caught on. He did really tacky things, like putting his wife in the magazine, publishing nude specials on Kimberley Conrad well after they were married. This seemed a bit creepy and tasteless, even if you thought of yourself as worldly. The *Playboy* lifestyle, of satin sheets and mirrored ceilings placed above gigantic circular beds whose headboards were loaded with electronic push-button whatevers, wasn't embraced by anybody I knew, and in anecdote only by a kind of greaseball set or nerdy losers. Besides, you couldn't have black satin sheets if you still lived at home. And when we got our first apartments, the idea of the circular bed seemed absurd, especially when we realized we'd be sleeping alone in it at least ninety-nine per cent of the time. I remember a guy named Bruce who sported an ascot to high school, an affectation he could only have picked up through the pages of *Playboy*. He seemed silly to us then, and he seems even more so when I think back to him now.

Other things about the magazine made you cautious. You never trusted the mental or emotional health of girls who were quoted saying they first saw *Playboy* in their father's tool sheds and there and then decided they some day wanted to be a centrefold. You never believed, and in fact probably found a bit frightening, the women who appeared in the magazine declaring that their mothers fully supported them.

Even as fetishism it was weak. Compared to what the Europeans were getting from, say, Helmut Newton in magazines as mainstream as French *Vogue*, *Playboy*'s girls on their garden swings seemed a bit insipid. Besides, the media, particularly advertising, was rapidly homing in on the sexy image. Sexually suggestive pictures were soon so pervasive we didn't need to go to taboo sources to be titillated. Before long, the models in a Sears catalogue were seen as more sexy than *Playboy*'s Playmates. Which is sort of the point: as our world grew ever more visual, fashion (or, more broadly, all advertising) photography became the next pornography, bombarding us until our senses became hopelessly dulled by overexposure. In the end, we outgrew the *Playboy* aesthetic.

Still, we couldn't avoid or resist the magazine's pull. *Playboy*, for men of my generation, governed our culture and a large part of our vocabulary – visual and verbal – concerning the female body, beauty, and sex. Any North American man who is forty or fifty will have had his image of sex and his fantasies during his teenage years strongly influenced, if not created, by Hugh Hefner. And if he denies that, he is lying. It was fantasy, true. There was a great gap between the illusions presented and the reality we had to deal with. Real sex (if we had it) was almost always messy, clumsy, groping. Ultimately more comic than cool. And it was far from a sure thing; hours of longing and frustration outnumbered moments of opportunity. Yet in *Playboy*, sex was never portrayed as messy – either physically or emotionally. And it was always a "sure thing."

Looking at *Playboy*, at least from a male point of view, should have been one of those rites of passage that we could grow out of and move on from, no harm done. You realized after a while that you weren't really going to learn anything about sex in its pages. And you would learn precious little that was reliable about anatomy. The exaggeration and airbrushing rendered pretty much everything unreal. *Playboy*'s girl next door never lived next door to me.

But *Playboy* did contribute, at least, that one very substantial thing to our sexual culture: the idea of variety with regularity. If monotony threatened to set in, the monthly Playmate kept hope and anticipation alive. The transition from one to the next was as easy as making a trip to the newsstand. This could not help but have a profound effect on our thinking. In young men, it teased attitudes and fixed expectations. And I believe it affected the rest of our lives. Once you grasp the appeal of an adolescence of infinite possibilities, you are locked likewise into a neverending adolescence. In my forties, I am single and so are at least half of the men (and more than half of the women) I know. We are still single or, more likely, single again in a lifelong journey that involves continuous manoeuvring into and out of and then back into romantic relationships. One of the profound social and cultural revolutions of the last half of this century is in the length (or shortness) of human sexual relationships, and the ease with which we, by and large, move on to form new ones. Ever optimistic. The last thirty years have been decades of high rates of divorce, transitory relationships, casual promiscuity (dangerous sexually transmitted diseases notwithstanding), and the invention of the quaint term "serial monogamy."

Let's for a moment suspend the standard judgement that these are all bad things. Let's just recognize that, good or bad, they stand out among the realities of modern life. And then let's think about how things got to be this way. Our mobility, our affluence, the pervasiveness of advertising, an overabundance of stimulation, choice, and possibility have all played their parts. As, no doubt, has our reluctance to ever consider ourselves satisfied. But if we recognize that these are now undeniable facts of life, we'll be able to understand how Hugh Hefner helped them along. We'll understand the magnitude of Hefner's and *Playboy*'s contribution to a huge sea change in the culture of this (sometime) puritan continent. We might acknowledge his place in North American culture only grudgingly, but nonetheless that place is substantial.

12

Dating at Midlife

There are 43 million single women in the United States, and over eight million who are single, widowed, or divorced in Canada. The numbers of single men are a bit fewer, possibly because we don't live as long. But the dramatic news: for the first time, 1990s census statistics in both the United States and Canada show that more people between the ages of thirty and sixty are single and living alone, than are part of couples. This is almost a doubling since 1971, and the numbers are growing at a rate double that of general population growth. What's more, the statisticians and demographers tell us something else: all of us – men and women – even if we get married or are married now, are likely to spend more than half of our adult lives single.

H.L. Mencken believed that the happiest people in the world were married women and single men. This opinion, which seems to have been based pretty much on intuition, came some sixty years before conductors of more scientific studies arrived at essentially the opposite conclusion. In the 1980s and 1990s, studies showed the suicide rate of single men was twice as high as that of married men; single men were far more likely to suffer nervous breakdowns, to be treated for depression, and to experience other psychological maladies such as insomnia and nightmares. Women, by contrast, were said to be happier single, especially as they grew older. They had superior friendships and support systems and lived more successfully alone. In this scheme of things, marriage seemed to be twice as beneficial to men as to women, in terms of both mental health and physical survival. Unmarried men died sooner than those married. Unmarried women lived longer than their married sisters.

However, this clear picture was soon muddied. In the late 1990s, Dr. Sagar Parikh, an expert in mood disorders at Toronto's Clarke Institute of Psychiatry, pointed out that "studies that associate male depression with marriage status confuse correlation with cause. Because two conditions are linked does not mean one causes the other." Bachelorhood could lead to depression. But it could be also the other way around: depressed men don't get married. Or something else altogether could be causing both male depression and bachelorhood. Another study (a mental-health supplement to the 1994 Ontario Health Survey) made the argument moot by discovering no significant difference between the percentage of single people (men and women) suffering from mental illness and that of married people.

I am one of these people who is single at middle age. This was not foreseen or deliberate; I believe I gave marriage a good try. My first marriage lasted for most of my twenties. A second, in my mid-thirties, didn't last very long, and might best be described as wishful thinking triumphing briefly over common sense. But being divorced and single are now two of my realities, realities that I don't at all feel badly about. And they are the realities of a good number of people I know. I used to belong to an informal club that included my upstairs neighbour, Ann; her friend, Paul; and a handful of other people. To be in the club you had to have been divorced at least twice. You had to have that bit of personal history. How much times have changed was shown by how easy it was to find people to join our club (three decades ago, you would have had to go to Hollywood to find such a cohort) and by the lack of shame we felt about our status. Not so long ago, someone with two divorces would have been seen as an abject failure. Now, blessedly, such a history is just road wear. Or mileage.

Since we were not only single, but lived far away from our parents or siblings or homes, we also had a group called "people without families." We would join together for Thanksgiving and Christmas festivities. At Christmas we would joke that the season had been invented by families to punish single people for having a better time the rest of the year.

The idea that we believed we had a better time the rest of the year is important. If you have to be single, this is possibly the best time in all of history to go solo. One of the markers of our times is the way being single has become acceptable, even normal. Society accommodates us single people in ways that it did not do for unattached people a generation or two ago, or really at any time throughout history. You can't find the words "bachelor" and "spinster" in common usage any more. Partly because there are so many of us, there has been no choice; all the elements of our culture and economy have had to jump to the response. Industries, from real estate to entertainment to tourism, more and more treat this demographic of single, middle-aged women and men as normal. The person renting a car, buying a condo, or travelling abroad is not made to feel an oddball for doing so alone. You can eat dinner and go to the theatre all by yourself quite happily, and without censure.

But you don't *have* to go to the theatre or eat dinner by yourself. Nor, according to some, should you. Despite the "normalizing" of single people and the acknowledgement of the substantial demographic we make up, a powerful assumption manages still to rule us, which is that, though at the moment we might be single, ultimately we want to pair up, or at least play the game of trying to pair up. Which brings us to the phenomenon of middle-aged dating.

Little did I imagine, when I was eighteen and twenty and going out on dates, that I would be doing the same thing when I was forty or forty-five or forty-eight. Yet here I am. Had I been able to foresee it, I'm sure I would have viewed it as somewhat bizarre. But now it doesn't seem bizarre at all. It's actually something I do with a fair amount of enthusiasm.

To date in your forties is the old dating, but also the new dating. Not much has changed, yet everything has changed. What's interesting is the tension between the old, deeply ingrained desires and assumptions, and the new realities – including everybody's heavier baggage and repertoires of cautions. To date in your forties definitely requires the invention of some new rules and the recognition of a few realities. There are some miles on the tires and the engine. There are different things to watch for, things that even the complete romantic, who believes anything is possible and any obstacle can be overcome, ignores at his peril.

By the time we are in our forties, both men and women fall into a couple of categories which are crucial to acknowledge and understand. These are:

You either have children, or you don't

and

Your past experiences have been essentially good ones, or they have been bad

Where you stand vis-à-vis these affects everything. When you're in your forties it's quite possible that you have kids who are already in their twenties. Or it's possible you have no children but have the potential and harbour a strong desire. In one week I went out with two different women, one whose biological clock was ticking loudly as she desperately searched for a relationship that would allow her to have her first child. The other had just become a grandmother. There was a two-year difference in their ages. A man who has children off at university had better have a very serious talk with himself should he catch himself interested in dating a woman who has no children, but nurtures hope.

Similarly, if you have more than one date with someone who has children, you are already involved with more than one person. A friend of mine fell head-over-heels for a woman with a twelve-year-old son. My friend had to expend a great deal more energy winning over the affections of the boy than scoring with his mother. And after a year of trying, he's not sure he's really there. The logistics of it went far beyond simply acknowledging that babysitters were required. For the first several months of the romance, whenever the son was home, my friend had to sleep on the couch. The twelve-year-old would not tolerate anybody sleeping with his mother.

The other category, people who have good as opposed to bad experiences on their curricula vitae, is even more complicated. And equally important. Children are among the tangible evidences of the life the person you might date has had before you. But there are lots of other things you can't see, many more than there might have been twenty years ago. By our forties, our tabula is not rasa; the carte is not blanche. We have already had long lives. Things have happened to us. Attitudes, ways of behaving, expectations, are set deeply. So are neuroses or psychoses. Other people's shoulders carry chips that you had nothing to do with putting there. The older you get, the more you are required to pay for the misdeeds of others of your sex.

For a moment we'll leave aside the midlifeman who is having a life crisis and deals with it by dumping his wife so that he can date – in his newly acquired red sports car – somebody more the age of his children. By and large, forties dating, to my pleasant surprise, is about quite mature things. Sex is still important. In the same way that a man's ambition for achievement is fuelled now by his awakened and growing sense of his mortality, so is his desire for sex. It is, again, the last kick at the can; no matter how many magazine articles we read about sex after seventy, it's the sex before seventy we're concerned about. I can't imagine any man (or woman) being contented with a sexless forties. That said, however, I don't think that in one's forties sex is nearly as critical to romance as it was when we were younger. It's not that we don't want it or like it, but there is a patience or a perspective wrapped around both behaviour and desire that certainly I didn't have when I was twenty. It's rumoured that after the first couple of months on the market, prescriptions for the erection drug, Viagra, dropped off precipitously. Middle-aged men apparently realized they didn't want as much sex as they had thought they would.

The other thing that is not nearly as important as it might seem is the matter of whether you are going to marry or live together. I went out for quite a long time with a woman who wanted us to act like a traditional couple only on weekends and when travelling. That suited me just fine; after ten years, more or less, on my own, I wasn't necessarily keen to rejig my laundry habits. At an earlier age, pairing-off or mating is a

critical end, the whole point of dating. Yet later in life –
maybe in large part because we don't have to think so much
about creating a nest in which to bring up offspring – we
seem able to understand that dating for its own sake is pleasant. We want to fill specific rather than general gaps in our
lives; we need to address only our need for company or our
loneliness. Or our needs for something interesting and stimulating. After forty, the romantic notion of "happily ever
after" that governs our culture still has power, but it is muted
by that fact that we are too smart, too experienced, maybe too
cynical (though I hope not) to buy it hook, line, and sinker.
We are, above all, pragmatists. Even exclusivity or monogamy
isn't as big an issue as it might have been when we were
younger. In our forties, we can be happy to see one another
while living separately and carrying on independent lives.
The things that are important (and better) about dating in
one's forties are the senses of companionship and friendship.
Talking, sharing pleasures, enjoying company, having the
minds meet – as well as the bodies.

But how do we get there? How do we go about doing it?
What happens when we find we must paddle (or that we are
still paddling) our middle-aged beings out from the quiet
shallows and back into the swift, unpredictable currents of
midstream? What bits of ourselves are we going to risk
putting on the line yet again? What will happen to us? How
will we fare? What is dating like for the majority of us who at
some time will, yet again, have to do it?

One crisp autumn Saturday morning I found myself on

the phone doing something I still consider weird. I was not talking, but listening. I'd dialed a number a friend, in an off-hand, joking, bet-you'll-never-go-there manner, had told me about. And I soon found myself listening to the voices of various women reading ads, or rather a series of ads like the following:

"If you saw me on the street, you'd probably take a second look. No, I'm not beautiful, but I am striking and exotic looking. I'm white, slender, five foot eight, with long, dark-brown hair and brown eyes, of Italian descent. I'm bright and funny, warm and loving, and sometimes totally impossible. You are very youthful, over forty-five – as am I – definitely single, hopefully over five foot eight, nice looking, cerebral, quick-witted, a non-conformist with strong values, and you haven't lost touch with your inner child. And you're full of curiosity, enthusiasm, and passion. That's what I am, and that's what I need. One thing more: I'm really only interested in dating, not a casual encounter."

Or the next:

"I want to meet a man who makes me feel like we've known each other forever. I'm forty-one with chin-length auburn hair, dimples, pretty green eyes, a beautiful smile, and a medium build. I'm told I'm youthful, but to be honest I wouldn't want to be any younger. You are family-oriented and loyal, open-minded and funny. Probably not a suit. Someone who likes independent and feisty women but can see the little girl inside. Someone who'll listen to Jane Siberry with me. I like *The X-Files*, Led Zeppelin, *Harper's Magazine*,

CBC Radio, *Due South*, glaciers, Thai food, hiking, camping, and people who aren't what they seem. I'm a combination of artsy, sophisticated, and small-town girl, I guess. I'm very liberal minded and I like a man with a wicked imagination, but one who's monogamous and affectionate."

At another time in my life I would never have imagined doing this. But here I was. I was setting up in a new city, eager to expand the horizons of both my social life and my romantic life. I needed to meet new people around my age and people who were in perhaps a similar situation.

The idea of meeting itself didn't bother me; I've always liked getting acquainted with women. The great thing about our times is that because there are so many middle-aged single people, there are infinite possibilities, especially in a city, to do so. I was finding that every time I turned around – at the gym, at work, in the laundry room of my building – a single woman seemed to be present. Eye contact could happen almost whenever I wanted it to: when stepping off the subway or hurrying down the street, or wherever else I might be – at church, the symphony, ball games. It was easy to get the impression that, should I wish to make a move and actually screw up the moxie to do so, my overture would be well received. As was the case back when I was eighteen years old, or twenty.

But the other thing about modern life is that if informal means of meeting don't work, there are more deliberate ways. Invention has followed necessity; there is no end of systems to help us out. Once a month, on a Wednesday evening, my city's major public museum offers a guest speaker putting forth on some weighty topic. But the event is called "Connecting for Singles," which tells you what it's really about. An intellectually respectable meet (meat) market. Or we could get technical. You can meet people over the Internet, through special categories of advertising in almost every newspaper, or through telephone services like the one I was trying out, which burgeon in greater numbers every week. The systems are almost universal; I found them in London, I found them in New York, they had them where I used to live in the middle of the continent, in Winnipeg. They proliferate in Toronto. They are ingenious forms of adventure, our traditional horror of blind dates notwithstanding. (They also must be enormously profitable for the companies that run them.) You can leave messages for total strangers and have them call you back. Your anonymity (and possibly your person) is protected initially by code numbers and recorded messages. But if you agree to get beyond that, a couple of hours later you can be sitting in some Starbucks feeling as awkward as you were when you were seventeen.

These services are not on some periphery reserved for oddballs. They are mainstream. To give some idea of the number of people wanting and availing themselves of them, a telephone system in Toronto called Telepersonals (available in a number of cities) had, when I checked, 3,513 ads from women seeking to meet men (1,100 from men wanting women). This, I figured, meant that about one out of every two hundred women in Toronto had advertised herself. In the preceding forty-eight hours, eighty-four new ads had been placed by women aged thirty-six to fifty-five. A little arithmetic told me that in a year this would work out to 15,372 requests from women in my age group alone. A good-sized town of women, all available and hoping for a date. And this on only one of many services.

That Saturday morning, I ploughed into the ads. For as long as I could stand listening, I clicked through them. They wanted: chemistry and communication, integrity, men who were open, reliable, good looking, at least six feet tall. One asked only for "a winner": "Are there any winners left out there?" Another explained her philosophy as Tom Cochrane's "Life Is a Highway." Just about everybody else claimed to be down-to-earth, fit, liking long walks on the beach, and prone to fine dining. A walk on the beach, a fine meal, and a good bottle of wine would seemingly make ninety per cent of these ad-placers happy. Occasionally, requests came up for "a man who is well endowed."

Were you an anthropologist, here would be the place to start your study of many cultural groupings: people at midlife, single people, mating habits, operating beliefs. And because I was listening only to ads placed by women between thirty-six and fifty-five, it gave me an incredible window on the life and culture of midlife or early middle age.

What I found required the most adjustment was the fact that a different set of hooks was being used to catch my interest. All my life I had responded visually; the first impression had always been given by someone's looks. But here the impression was made first by the voice, leaving the mind to form a picture. To get a visual image, all you can do is take the word of the person at the other end of the line, let the imagination work, and hope for the best. I found myself attracted to tones of voice and accents.

There were also ads that veered from the beaten path. All kinds of possibilities were offered in this supermarket.

"I am a thirty-seven-year-old professional, married, black female, five foot two inches tall and a hundred and ten pounds. I am interested in meeting a tall male between thirty-eight and forty-five for an old-fashioned romantic love affair. You must be physically fit and I stress, physically fit, mentally stimulating, clean, and above all, be in control of your own life."

One, mincing no words, offered this: "I'm looking for a bright, fortysomething man who is down-to-earth and would enjoy outings to theatres or restaurants with a chic, five-foot-seven redhead. Please, no lawyers or liars."

Then there were the interesting ones: "I thoroughly enjoy not enjoying corporal punishment" one voice explained. "Are you a man that understands that?"

Or: "I am an extremely sensual and sexual forty-year-old woman who's looking to find a clean, straight man, someone passionate, creative, fit, articulate, and gentlemanly who'd like to give me pleasure and take his pleasure with me while my lover watches."

Okay, what was I going to do? I thought once more about how loath I would have been at any earlier time in my life to pursue something like this. I considered what my attitude would have then been toward the "desperate"people who did so. Then my curiosity and perhaps my sense of adventure got the better of me. I thought about my obligations as a researcher. In the interests of science, I paid for a membership and started responding to ads. "Hello, my name is Larry . . ."

I felt more the anthropologist than the lover, but nonetheless understood the importance of putting my best foot forward. Pronouncing myself "fit and attractive" to total strangers didn't come easy. Nor should it. Yet pretty soon I found myself beyond the message stage. My phone was ringing. Women for whom I'd left my number were calling back for in-depth chats. Then, like an automaton in a script where there's no turning back, I was slapping on aftershave and heading off to the art gallery to see if I'd recognize some woman named Catherine – and she me – by the descriptions we'd exchanged. In the back of my mind was the nagging worry: how in the world would we escape if it became apparent on first sighting that this was all a big mistake?

Catherine threw me off balance right away by telling me that wasn't her real name; it was just a sort of nom de telephone. She also said meeting in an art gallery was a bad idea because her former husband was an artist. So we got out straight away and went to a nearby coffee shop. Catherine (I found it very hard to shift from thinking of her as Catherine, which probably doomed us) was the vice principal of an elementary school; she liked to ski and had been recently to Austria. She had nice hands.

During my "study," I found that none of the women I met were psychological basket cases; they were, I thought, kind of like me. Most of them looked pretty much the way they had described themselves. But I heard a number of stories about men who didn't live up to the billings they'd given: bald men had claimed to have hair; five foot three and portly had promoted themselves as tall, slim, and fit. Married guys said they were single; fifty-year-olds tried to pass themselves off as thirty-five. Men who said they had professions turned out to be unemployed. At least that's what several soured and perplexed women told me. "What's the percentage in lying?" I asked. "Didn't they expect you'd figure it out when you saw them?"

The women, as I said, were not like this. They looked good. If they had a weakness, it was that they were romantics. They wanted love and they wanted it soon. But this was not about love; this was about meeting. Love, if ever, would have to be much later.

At some point everybody has to understand that the technical introduction is just that: an introduction. From there, you are on your own just as you would be in any of the old, traditional methods of encounter – a train, a crowded party, walking out of church. The disappointed people are those who advertise not to have a first meeting with someone who is single and might have some common interests, but who ask for a soulmate and feel they don't have time to settle for anything less. I spoke to a few of these – women who were bound to be disappointed by wanting to jump past all the intermediate steps of dating. Nevertheless, most people had an abundance of sanity and good humour. In a bit of a throwback, almost every meeting elicited the obligatory disclaimer, "I don't normally do this." To seek a mate, a friend, a date in this manner seems to most people just a little bit . . . less. They think it carries an element, however tiny, of shame. Conversations were built around justification, about how, in the absence of other methods, it isn't really so bad, and around plausible fictions, things we might tell friends should we ever have to explain how we met. In almost every mind was this grim thought: Am I so desperate I had to advertise?

But they did advertise. And that's one of the realities of the new dating. So who's to fault it? If it's happening so much, it must be normal. If being single at midlife is now normal, then so, surely, are the other things that go with it.

After a while, though, it wore me out. I was relieved and happy when, at a chamber-music concert, I met a bright, attractive woman who read books and who I wanted to see (and she me) more than twice. I stepped out of the rat race and settled down, so to speak. Relieved. Too much dating had caused the kind of ennui that settles in when you are travelling and live too long out of a suitcase. I was happy to leave it behind.

If old acerbic, insightful Mencken were around today, would he find us single men and women happy and mentally healthy? Who's to say? Or he might be surprised by which of us are happy and which are not. And for what reasons. Perhaps we're never happy for more than a few minutes anyway.

Perhaps what makes us believe we are happy and healthy is simply a sense of our possibilities. Even in medieval times there were popular sayings about how those not married wished they were, while those married wished they weren't. Maybe the best we can say is that now, for a rare moment in history, the matter of choice concerning our personal lifestyle is wide open – with all the stress that carries. And for that we should feel lucky.

13

Trying to Understand Women Trying to Understand Men Trying to Understand How to Keep It All Going

Men don't understand women, and they know it.
Women don't understand men, and they don't know it.

— GAIL SHEEHY

A friend of mine, Marilyn, tells me her summer reading is a book called *Women Who Love Too Much*.

"Sounds steamy," I say, imagining a page-turner to take to the beach.

She laughs. "It's not a novel. It's a relationship book."

"Oh."

I wince.

Let me say, right off the bat, that Marilyn is not a helpless slave to anything other than rationality. She's a completely able human being, a tough lawyer who, just the week before, put a murderer away for life. And it's not just Marilyn. Some of the smartest women I know, three more lawyers and a college teacher for starters, are unabashed consumers of relationship-help books. It's not that they have one which lasts them a lifetime, like the home medical dictionary, or keeping going with *Leaves of Grass* or *The Prophet* long after graduation from college; they'll buy a new tome every couple of months. The word travels like wildfire. The books are purchased six at a time and given to friends. "You need to read . . ." Sometimes they want to give them to men. "Maybe (since he's giving you so much grief) you should get him to read . . ." In Marilyn's case, she's bought copies for three of her friends and then says maybe I'd like to read it.

I'm not about to read it. I'm a man. Men don't read self-help books (unless they're about making money, and maybe not even then). In one of our bibles, *Esquire* magazine, on a list of things cool men mustn't do, Number 58 was "don't read self-help books." And Number 59 commanded "don't date, befriend, or converse with anyone who reads self-help books." This was just a little above the Number 73 admonition: "don't pretend to like Robert James Waller (even to get laid.)"

Not all women buy these books, I should hasten to add; another friend, Stephanie, sniffs and warns me not to put her in that category. "We don't learn to live from self-help books," says Stephanie. "To find the deeper truths you need to read poetry, look for the multiple layers in art. Give it time." An attitude I respect. "But most people," she goes on, "are product-oriented. They think these books somehow will produce the product."

A relationship is different from dating. Dating skills and single-living skills are not relationship skills. Dating is just shopping and walking around; a "relationship," the ability to manage something that's long term and mutually invested, is a different ball game. I watch with awe and envy people who I believe do it well. I make notes, with self-interested fascination, on others who struggle (not always successfully) with trying to do it well. Yet, after all these years, I realize mostly how much I don't know. And what a huge mystery it all still remains.

A great deal has been made about what we believe to be the differences between men and women, as if these might account for something. Some explainers set up binary systems with men at one pole and women at the other, like the posts on the battery in your car, between which only a charge can go. Other analogies have us originating on different planets. I think the binary systems are essentially bunk. Human desires and motivations can't possibly be that far apart. But at the same time, regardless of what men and women might possess in common, there is still a river to cross. Which means bridges must be built. If there is a gender split, perhaps that split is in how we go about looking at and trying to build and maintain those bridges. And perhaps it has to do with the tools we choose to use.

The sort of dismissiveness men feel toward relationship books is the first sign of our suspicions of the women's bridge-building methods. As well as a sure sign that we are nervous. We are put on alert and go into a defensive mode.

The subplot is serious. What our lovers, wives, women friends are really trying to do here, we figure, is find out why they've never ended up with what they believe to be the right man. Or if not that, then how to make the man they do have behave himself or change into something they like better. Both of these, of course, are unsettling thoughts. We fear there is trickery in the wind. We suppose first, in the same way we sometimes suspect women are suckers for tea-cup and Tarot card readers, that women are being tricked by the simplistic irrationality of the prescriptions. Then, we believe, the tricks will be turned on us. And in our usual manner when dealing with women, we won't then know what to do. We suspect that women are preparing one of two things. They are either preparing to leave us, or they are getting help figuring out how to change us. Neither of these is something we will be very happy about. The evidence is blatant; the titles confirm this. On the leaving front, a couple of titles currently on the relationship shelves are: *The Language of Letting Go* and *When Love Is Not Enough*. On the changing-your-man front, a book prominently displayed currently is Michele Weiner-Davis's *A Woman's Guide To Changing Her Man: Without His Even Knowing It*. A title sure to give pause to the male half of the population.

Women Who Love Too Much, by Robin Norwood (which sold like hotcakes) goes a step past this. Its justifying premise states: "When you keep wishing and hoping he'll change." This tells you that you must learn how to cut your losses when the hoped-for changes are not forthcoming. (The woman who loves too much is the woman who is too stupid to quit.)

Realizing someone is trying to change or fix him is an exceedingly worrying thing for a man. In response, we believe we must be wary, like superpowers continuously eyeing one another's nuclear arsenals. All of mythology tells us to be on guard. We will not forget poor Samson, whose strength was shorn by Delilah while he slept. Or Enkidu, in the epic of Gilgamesh, who is enticed by woman in the form of a harlot and watches his masculinity and his independence dissipate as he is "tamed."

Men might, if caught at a good moment, be grudgingly willing to acknowledge we possess faults requiring work. But it's the idea of any manipulation from outside that is profoundly irritating. We are very thin-skinned about this. I experienced a flash of defensiveness when a woman I was dating made the simple comment that I should use a different brand of olive oil and asked how could I operate a kitchen without having a mill to grind fresh pepper? She was right; I knew this immediately. The advice was both harmless and useful. But that didn't stop the moment of defensiveness when I thought my kitchen, simple and badly stocked as it was, was about to be changed.

Another highly perplexing thing for a man is to realize how the ground shifts once he is in a relationship with a woman. His strengths suddenly become his faults. The thing about him that initially most appealed to his loved one is now the characteristic that she is most vehemently criticizing. Women often think this is funny. A popular cabaret show making the tour recently was called *I Love You, You're Perfect, Now Change*. Men are appalled. Or we should be. We may be stubborn, but we think consistency is a virtue. I was in a lengthy relationship with a woman who told me early that what appealed to her was my sense of independence and adventure. Eighteen months later, you can guess which of my qualities were causing her the most irritation and grief.

Among ourselves, men make feeble stabs at explaining the mysteries of what can make relations with women sing, and then freely admit how much we don't understand. To women we admit less, because we're always looking for a leg to stand on, and admitting too much might take that away. We do understand some of the rudiments of negotiation. Beyond that, I think we remain endlessly fascinated, though tirelessly wary.

We men resent what we believe to be women's presumption that they have us all figured out. In turn, we have some of our own rules. One of them is, if you don't tell anybody about it, it didn't happen. But maybe the biggest difference is in our use of the word itself, "relationship." Men rarely use that word to define either what we have or what we'd like. That R-word has always been female. I asked a number of my friends and all of them agreed they never initiate the term into conversation; they use it only in response, and only reluctantly at that. A relationship is a process, a struggle that is ongoing. Women have processes. Men don't. Men have objects: friends, girlfriends, wives, families, children, lovers. Jobs, cars, houses. We know what objects are and we know about the campaigns to get them. Find it, buy it, and bag it. Processes are foreign to us; they take too long. The R-word men seem to prefer is "results."

Men often possess the view that what we have with our female partners is likely to work best the same way our car or our lawnmower or our house works, through attention to small details. Kind of a Tim "the Toolman" Taylor *Home Improvement* approach. My friend Gregg, who believes he coined the term, thinks of himself as an eavestrough- or gutter-cleaner, and attributes the success of his ten-year marriage to that talent. This has a double meaning, of course; it describes an actuality, and it is a metaphor. Men have to know how to go about the multitude of chores that keep their family's houses and garages and cottages from falling into rot and disrepair. Our dads taught us this. There is a lengthy tradition of men believing that if the plumbing works everything else will be okay. You must keep your car or your lawnmower tuned. The understanding, when converted to metaphor, is that it is often the failures of small shared things that start to get couples down. Thus the enterprise of gutter-cleaning metaphorically keeps open the channels so that the water continues to flow, so that the metaphorical drain works after a metaphorical heavy downpour. So that the metaphorical roof doesn't leak or rot and the not-so-metaphorical relationship will continue to stay dry and happy. There is probably not nearly as much distance between what men want and what women want as the sceptics would have us think. It is not the case that men don't want to work at relationships. Maybe we just do it using a different language.

But this theory of maintenance only goes so far. It doesn't help us when something big happens. You can keep the oil changed in your car, but some day the clutch might give out. Or the transmission. What do you do then?

Some of our biggest problems can show up well on in the lifespan of a relationship, like now, when we are at midlife. Marriages that have been maintained for a long time through attention to details can suddenly face big changes in direction.

A couple I know who've been married for fifteen years recently booked themselves what was billed as a cozy weekend at a country inn. They had no sooner made the reservation, however, than a sort of panic set in. It turned out that although they had been married for fifteen years, more than thirteen of those years had passed since they'd been anywhere alone together. Just the two of them. The whole of their life had been centred around their children. They shared the load and the task of being parents beautifully and successfully, but suddenly they were less than certain about other things. They were genuinely terrified, the friend who'd recommended the inn found out when she talked to them.

The wife asked all the questions. The husband, a quiet fellow prone to speaking only after carefully choosing his words, was off somewhere else keeping a sort of nervous, self-contained silence. We don't know if she was speaking for both of them or only herself. But what, she demanded, were they supposed to do once they got to the inn? How were they to fill their days and evenings? This question was asked in such a way that the second half remained delicately unstated, and that was – "when it was just the two of them and they were all alone."

Lurking in the wings of every relationship, I believe, is our first great fear: that we won't be able to keep it going. In the naïveté of youth we believe – or at least I did – that marriage might kind of take care of that. Once the marriage vows had been said, you could relax. You could (figuratively at least) forget to shave for a couple of days. You were safe; it was a done deal. However, two divorces have disabused me of that notion. I now know I can take nothing for granted; the challenge to keep things going is always with us.

Our other great fear concerns the mystery of relationships. We long for explanations and formulae, we search for guaranteed ways to make sure everything is always great. But our (legitimate) fear is that there are no real answers; no explanations for either the failures or, for that matter, the relationships that work. That marvelous quality we call "chemistry," which makes things sing when we first meet someone we really like and when we fall in love, transmutes into something that remains un-nameable and unfathomable. There is no recipe, there is no code. Like me, many men reach middle age with the whole topic of relationships still solidly in the sphere of "mysteries."

By the time we're in our forties, one thing we men should have learned is that the bottom-line decisions in relationships between men and women are nearly always made by women. Have you ever noticed how even in strong patriarchal cultures, where women appear to have few formal powers, mothers, wives, even daughters take for granted their ability, through a mere look, to turn the menfolk to jelly? In the informal institutions of the home, the marketplace, even the non-altar sections of the church, women rule. And since formal society is built on top of the informal institution of home and family, the most significant shots have already been called by women even in those societies that appear male-centred. The wives of Athens realized that all it would take to bring an end to the twenty-seven-year-long Peloponnesian War was their refusal to have sex with their husbands. For the male erection drug, Viagra, to work, it's said a man should take it one hour before having sex. Which caused comedian Jay Leno to quip that the only person who knows an hour ahead if there's going to be sex is the woman.

The place where men and women come together and most need each other – and therefore where we ought to be able to make the most common cause – is sex. But this is the biggest mystery of all. Do we have any idea what our common needs, male and female, are here? And how common are they? What are our basic assumptions about our sexual needs, our partner's sexual needs, and where sex fits in our relationships? The great dance all our life is about trying to get what we want and trying to learn how to get what we want. But there's a world of things we might not have thought much about. We are filled with assumptions, but then we encounter a whole minefield of challenges to those assumptions.

In 1929, the philosopher Bertrand Russell wrote, in what must have been at the time a scandalous little book called

Marriage and Morals, "I think that uninhibited, civilized people, whether men or women, are generally polygamous in their instincts. They may fall deeply in love and be for some years entirely absorbed in one person, but sooner or later sexual familiarity dulls the edge of passion, and they begin to look elsewhere for a revival of the old thrill. It is, of course, possible to control this impulse in the interests of morality, but it is very difficult to prevent the impulse from existing." Russell was addressing the final great fear of relationships: Will we be able to sustain the sex? And if not, what will we do then? He suggested polygamy and legalized prostitution. (I think he envisioned only men as customers, though if he were writing today he might admit women, too.)

Bertrand Russell was a very smart man. But what we're listening to here is his profound unhappiness (almost as profound, according to his biographers, as the unhappiness of his poor wife). And if it is not a profound unhappiness for the rest of us, it is at least a lurking fear. Do we have it within us to regenerate something approximating sexual interest when we become bored or boring? Will that become a crisis that destroys our relationship? Will it provoke us to reconstitute our relationship? Or will we limp along, either sublimating or in denial, believing other habits and connections will be enough to carry us through? There is no end of prescriptions to address this question, some of them not much of an advance on Russell. The Real Women movement tries to persuade every wife to be a temptress, greeting her mate at the door in a negligee and offering a martini (not far from

Russell's prostitute). The (apparently) fast-growing swingers movement argues for consensual variety (Russell's polygamy). Magazine articles (and probably the relationship books) tell us to open dialogues with our partners, but leave us on our own to make our way through this terribly sensitive and dangerous area.

I am afraid I have no answers. I have only fears and questions. Even a guy like me who's proven he can survive divorces doesn't necessarily want to have any more of them. But neither do I want to live safe but half-dead. If love is killed when it is a duty and flourishes only when left to be free, how do we keep it and ourselves and one another free?

One hopeful thing Russell had to say was this: "An example of the mental peculiarity of human beings from which spring both their vices and their intelligence [is] the power of imagination to break up habits and initiate new lines of conduct." This is the real issue: finding the courage to look into ourselves and push into the next realm, when we need to, beyond comfort and habit and selfishness. I want the language of making things work. I want the imagination and the courage to go with my beloved *where* I might be afraid to go, whatever my fears might be. And to go there *when* I'm afraid to.

Our friends who had their weekend away at the cozy country inn are safely home again. There's a lot I don't know except that, unlike my friend and I who liked the inn and found it charming, they found a lot to complain about and spent part of their three days quarrelling with the inn-keeper. I'll leave it to you to interpret what that might mean. Now, they seem relieved. Relieved to be back in the world that includes their house and neighbourhood, jobs and children. Relieved, no doubt, to have returned unscathed. I think it's too early to ask what they learned. I look at them and think them, in their own way, kind of brave. I know numerous couples at this stage of life who are secretly terrified about the impending moment when the kids leave; when something changes; when they will be booted out of their groove. This couple briefly, and in their own small way, ventured out. Beyond the pattern. Where the relationship is never a sure thing. I have to wish them well. I wish all of us well. And for the moment, at least, I'm happy to note that they survived.

14

For the first time in eleven years, Sarah will not be with me at Loon Cottage. At age eighteen she is off navigating some river system in the northwest Ontario wilds that even the best of my maps shows as inaccessible except by canoe or float plane. The thing I've always liked about Canada is the way it's possible get on an airplane at some southern airport and, with a turn north, be almost immediately beyond tangible evidences of civilization. Looking out the porthole when aloft and seeing the rocky and treed wilderness below, the thought occurs that if you keep flying you mightn't spy any agglomeration of lights or pavement or cleared land again until you reach, say, Moscow. I've always found such thoughts not disturbing but immensely comforting. It's as if I need regularly to be assured there's still lots of world left.

For six weeks, my daughter and eight other young women, two of them experienced leaders, will be taking canoes into this primordial wilderness. They will eat dehydrated foods, sleep on the ground, shoot white-water rapids. Her mother and I and the other parents have been given itineraries meant to help us keep abreast of their project and its progress. The pieces of paper are actually disconcerting in the frankness with which they present the daily events of our children's trip. The girls will lug their gear over more than a hundred portages. They are scheduled to see other humans only twice: when they stop for food and mail pick-ups at two isolated Indian trading posts along the Albany and Attawapiskat Rivers, rivers that flow northeast toward James Bay and Hudson Bay. They will be able to call home from Fort Hope (indeed) and Landsdowne House, into which they will paddle after week three and week five respectively. The base camp will be in contact with them the rest of the time only by radio phone and only in case of emergency: medical, accident, or forest fire. Sarah had to audition for this trip. The process was like applying for a job as an astronaut. She wanted desperately to be accepted, and when the acceptance came she was on top of the world. I'm very proud of her and her growing independence. I remember when I first offered her a paddle and waited to see how she would handle it in the stern of a canoe. Now she's going to be using one for six weeks. The longest canoe trip I ever made was three days.

My brother and his family arrive for a short visit. They – John and Hilda and my nephew and two nieces, three kids in their early teens – drove for three days to get here. They check in at the motel in Sioux Narrows because my little cottage isn't nearly large enough to accommodate five additional people. But for a couple of days, they spend the daytime hours with me. It feels good to be a host, even if I've never believed myself to be the world's most natural one. While the kids swim, we adults mix gin and tonic, listen to the birds, and look at the lake. Then we set up the barbecue.

To get here, my brother and his family have driven their minivan around the southern shores of three of the Great Lakes – Huron, Michigan, and Superior – through the heartland of America. It is one of those summer trips that pits families in vehicles against hundreds of miles of highways. They've seen a quarter of the continent flash past their tinted windows. They stopped for restaurants, theme parks, and hotels or motels with pools. They stopped for a ball game in Milwaukee, where the Brewers were playing Colorado and my nephew caught a ball popped to him by Chuck Finley. They followed the automobile association guidebooks and discovered how no stone has been left unturned in order to create a tourist draw. In Wisconsin, they traced their way through the Dells, a series of scenic islands and cliffs of richly weathered sandstone rock along the Wisconsin River. But immediately they discovered that these Dells also offered the Wax World of the Stars, the Pirate Cove, the Biblical Gardens, Crazy King Ludwig's Adventure Park, the Ho-Chunk

Casino. At Old River Adventure Golf, they stopped to play a round. In the town of La Crosse they marvelled at six silos full of beer: the World's Biggest Six Pack.

After stopping to see me, they will head on to a reunion of my sister-in-law's clan. Hilda's father, as a young boy, came from Russia, part of an emigration of Mennonites. Now her family, like so many others, is scattered across North America. Family has become a continental item. I know families that draw their three generations out of a variety of cities and communities from the Atlantic to the Pacific. To have children or parents or brothers and sisters close at hand is an increasing rarity. As North America is a continent of descendants, offspring of immigrants, the task for many, now, is to recall that decisive moment when the first generation left the Old World, and then to keep up their clan connections by driving hundreds or thousands of miles to participate in periodic reunions, just as Hilda is doing.

Almost all of us must remember being dragged to such events as children, to be presented to and confronted with people we hardly knew. But they were our kin. Our blood connections. They were people with whom we may have shared nothing at all save that most ephemeral (some would say profound) connection: a common ancestor and, at some point, a common story. Now we are doing the dragging. Family, we have come to realize, is not something that just "happens" on its own.

Now that we are in our forties, my brother, his wife, and I find that we have become the connective tissue between the generations. We have this special job, which is to make sure our children get their taste of the larger family. It's our job at midlife, just as my being host to my close family at the lake is my job. If we don't do these things now, when will we do them? At some point we have to become not only part of, but responsible for, the chain of tradition. That point, it seems, is now, at midlife. In conservative Jewish practice, the surviving child after the death of parents, through a process of mourning called Kaddish, tries to fulfil the obligations to the community that the deceased parent had. The chain of tradition can thus remain unbroken. You don't do things at this point in your life strictly for pleasure, but to fulfil the obligation of being the "between" generation. The young – like my daughter in her canoe – can go off on their adventures. The in-between generation has responsibilities. My brother and my sister-in-law, through this trip across the continent, will be connecting their children to their ancestors and their story.

Making these connections has become critically important to us. We look at our children and see how quickly they are growing up, how soon they will be independent, out of the nest, and gone off on their own perhaps to some other city. My nephew and nieces are fifteen, thirteen, eleven; it will happen in a flash. We look at our surviving parents, aunts, uncles, and realize how quickly they are aging. There is not much time in the middle. Not much time to do the job social and cultural history ordains us to do.

Last spring we had an eightieth birthday party for our mother. She protested she didn't want any fuss, but we wanted to have some kind of celebration in honour of this person who was always busy – when she was our age – honouring everybody else. Or looking after everybody else. My brother and I realize now, after we've had a chance to look at the real world, that our mother's life, raising us boys alone after our father died, wasn't easy. We thought it was high time we found some way to say thank you.

Through numerous long-distance phone calls, we managed to agree on arrangements. We invited every friend and relative and neighbour we could think of and asked them to come to an "open house" at the church in the community where our mother has always lived, and where my brother and I grew up. I took Sarah out of school for a couple of days, and we bought our airplane tickets early. We decorated the basement hall of the church with streamers and old photographs. We bought flowers and corsages. We ordered a cake.

On a Saturday afternoon they all came. Our mother, who has never wanted to be the centre of attention, stood in the middle of her family and friends and acquaintances who stretched back over three-quarters of a century and basked in it all. She didn't seem to mind in the end that she'd "let" us, her family, do this after all. She was grateful. But not so much as were we. We'd been permitted, after all, to do our job.

15

Parenting Our Parents

I grow old . . . I grow old . . .
I shall wear the bottoms of my trousers rolled.

— *T. S. ELIOT,*
The Love Song of J. Alfred Prufrock

My brother and I have decided to give our mother the nudge. After a great deal of agonizing we have convinced ourselves this is necessary. Our mother is eighty-two. She still lives in her house, drives her car, and tends her garden. With a bit of help from a man who comes once a week to cut the grass and do yard work, and a young woman (our mother refers to her as a "girl") who does the heavier housework and cleaning, she manages very well and is proud that she remains independent. All this is wonderful. But John and Hilda and I worry.

We want her to move into a retirement apartment. The one we have in mind is a charming, sprawling, burnt-red brick complex situated on the edge of a park, with delightful views of the passing river and a pond swimming with swans. It is not some warehouse shabbily put together and hidden away. It is less than a mile from where she lives now and is filled with people who are her friends. It has a charming name: Maple Terrace. We think it is ideal.

The possibility of making this move is not something entirely alien or undesirable to our mother. She thought of the idea herself and we are sure it has been part of her internal plan for a long time, sitting in the bank of down-the-road inevitability. She acknowledges consistently that she will do it. But the hitch is that she doesn't want to do it just yet. "I'm not ready," she says.

Which is the issue. Which is what makes us nervous. When will she be ready? We try to ease her along: "Yes, we know you might not be ready. But you have to get your name in. The waiting list is possibly two years long, and if you don't get your name in you will be out of luck when you actually do want and need to make such a move. Besides, if your name comes up and you're still not ready you can simply say so."

We tell ourselves that we worry lest our mother end up overwhelmed and helpless. To maintain a house all by oneself is a big responsibility. Winter, especially, is worrisome. In this part of the world they are long and severe. There is ice, there is snow, there is day after day of being shut in and lonely. But our worry is pasted over with something else, a thin veneer of unmistakable guilt. We are mired in a mix of motive that is half altruistic, half shamefully selfish. We are half sincerely

concerned with our mother's welfare, half preoccupied with
our own convenience. We fear perhaps more that it is we who
will end up overwhelmed and helpless.

The dialogue and the manipulation we catch ourselves
going through has a familiar ring. It is the reverse of the
parents and the twenty-year-old child. "Why aren't you
going to school? When are you going to get a job? Why don't
you try this one? At least go for an interview. Don't you think
it's time you considered moving out?" It's become clichéd to
say we catch ourselves turning into parents for our parents.
But if it weren't at least somewhat true, it wouldn't be a
cliché. It's the fate of almost all middle-aged persons. I, for
one, hate the role.

The extra edge, of course, is a more dreadful fear. We
realize how rapidly the next flip of the generations will
happen, and how soon it will be our children saying to us, in
only a blink after we have gone on at them about getting the
job and moving out, "Don't you think this house is getting to
be a bit much for you?" Years ago, when my grandparents
were getting old and their generation were passing away, I
overheard my uncle say to my mother, his sister, "Soon it will
be us who are the old people." When I was a boy, and my uncle
was the age that I am now, I worked for him on Saturdays and
school holidays. I remember how I was in awe of the sizable
business he ran and the success he enjoyed and the levers he
pulled and the employees he supervised. This uncle is now in
a nursing home and whenever he wants to make a move he
has to be helped by an attendant, lest he fall and hurt himself.

He can't even go to the bathroom by himself; the attendants have to pick him up like a doll to set him on the toilet. I might as well repeat his words to my brother: "Soon it will be us who are the old people."

When I visit my uncle and see the poor miserables who are his roommates, a despondency settles over me that doesn't lift for a day or more. Their reversion is complete; if our mother is moving to become the teenager whose life we feel we must organize, those poor souls are infants. Their handlers spout baby talk, and jolly Care Bears form the prevailing decorative motif to preside over what I can only think must be lonely, awful, boring days. Never have I seen or smelled such unhappiness and despair: old women curled in the fetal position on their beds or parked in wheelchairs, their spouses and friends dead or mere phantoms of memories lost in clouds of Alzheimer amnesia. Children and grandchildren are begged to come visit.

"Why don't you come to see me more often?"

"I've been here every day this week, you just can't remember."

"I think I saw my mother."

"She's been dead for thirty-five years."

I think I will ask to be shot rather than spend any time in such an existential purgatory. Perhaps my uncle's roommates, if given better voice, would ask the same. My mother is not like her brother; she is lucid and able and, with the exception of a hearing disability and a few sundry minor concerns, as healthy as any eighty-two-year-old I know. She has still the possibility of much life, life of the kind that she and we understand. But nevertheless, the change in relationship between her and us, her offspring, is new and unsettling.

My most guilty secret is having fantasies that our mother will die before she has to go into a nursing home. God knows I don't want her to die now. But a fervent hope for my mother, as for myself, is that the end, when it comes, will be before, rather than after, that dreadful last chapter. That she will pass quietly and painlessly while she is still on her game, in her house and with her garden and having played the organ yet one more time in her church. When life is to end, let it be some time like that. There have been occasions when I have been staying in her house, and we've had a good dinner and a game of Scrabble and the grandchildren have been there, all teenagers now, growing up and handsome and untroubled, and I wake up in the middle of the night and listen to the quiet and think: What if it happened tonight? And then I feel fiendish for allowing such a thought.

This all seems shabby. Such is the nature of this enterprise, not just the moving, but all aspects of this "taking over," that it's almost impossible to carry any part of it through without feeling ugly. No matter what we do or think, it's hard to feel any honour. All manipulation is like that. But in this hopeless shabbiness I am not alone; my generation are in league. Our mother might be at odds with us, but my brother and I have come together in complete agreement. And it's more than us; through anecdotal evidence I realize that every one of my friends is up to the eyebrows in the same story. It is the preoccupation of my generation, just as a short while ago rock and roll, sex, cars, political protest, and choosing daycare for our first child were. Having rationalized notions of what will be "good" for our parents, yet driven by fears of our own impending helplessness, the generation has united. It is a trauma that is still largely secret; hardly anybody talks about it voluntarily. Yet when you bring up the subject, everyone has a story.

Jay and Susanna tell me Wednesday will be a good night to meet for dinner at a favourite Greek restaurant because they will be downtown anyway at supper hour "looking after some business." I'm impressed. Of all my friends, Jay is the bona fide entrepreneur. He'll probably arrive at dinner owning a new company. But when they come in to the restaurant looking a bit worn, they announce they have been with Jay's mother. The "business matter," it turns out, was to make arrangements for the mother, who is seventy-six, to sell her suburban condo and move to a single-bedroom apartment in midtown. For a decade since selling the big family home, she has lived in the condo with Jay's father, who once was a prominent lawyer and a judge. He is now in a veteran's hospital, the victim of a series of strokes. He can't walk; he is confined to a wheelchair. He is lucid for periods but then can't remember when anyone last came to see him. He watches his favourite sport, golf, on television and appreciates a player's approach to the green. But if you ask who the leaders might be in the tournament, he becomes confused and can't remember. Still, he's in better shape than many others.

His floor is loaded with raving old guys who sometimes forget their own names. Everyone is grateful that he is not such a mess as they; but that also compounds the emotional turmoil. Jay's father seems able to express strongly only one emotion: anger. He is angry at his wife who won't let him live with her any more, he is angry at his family who put him where he is now, and he is angry at his body, which tricked him, and at his Presbyterian god, who offered him this life. When visited, the judge first becomes angry and then he cries. Which triggers the predominant emotion of his family. Guilt. Guilt that they put him there, guilt that they are helpless, too, to do anything else for their father, and guilt that his berth is so miserable. Jay sums up the family view: "He always provided well and looked after his family, now his family can't look after him."

Another friend, Nick, tells me he can't meet for a bite to eat on a certain night. Why not? He must take his turn at another hospital and feed dinner to his father. Another stroke. Another powerful man, once head of the municipal administration in a large city, reduced to a bed and a wheelchair. Almost deaf, unable to speak or read. The mocking images on television dance in front of fixed, uncomprehending eyes. He waits to be fed by the family that takes turns visiting him.

There are others. John, my age, waits for a space to open up in a care home for his mother, suffering for four years now from Parkinson's Disease.

What I note is how matter-of-fact all my friends are about these obligations. Or how little they say about them. Nick is one of my best friends, yet I didn't know for the longest time that supper on every fifth night at the chronic-care hospital was part of his ritual. We share a deep concern, a deep terror. We seldom talk about it.

It is an interesting thing, too, that these, my friends, are all men. Not to say that women don't worry about their parents or have a (probably still unfair) share of the load. But the men I know are not shirking or escaping. In some cultures, and even in ours as recently as when I was a child, one young woman in every family took on the care of elderly parents. My grandparents, who both lived into their eighties, were looked after by my Aunt Margaret, who never married. My other grandfather (my grandmother had died in middle age) was looked after into his eighties by a niece who also never married. Did these women sacrifice their lives? Or did the elderly parents provide shelter for those who would have been on their own otherwise? Either way, it was a system that doesn't function any more. Nor perhaps, should it. My mother has no daughter, and neither my brother nor I are likely to give up careers and independence to take care of her full-time. I don't want or expect my daughter to do so for me and am horrified to think the thought would even cross her mind. And yet what is our system? And what is our proper, honourable, human role when all the shit hits that fan?

The waiter at the restaurant brings our second bottle of a bitter red wine, perhaps chosen subconsciously to match our mood, and finally our entrees of grilled red snapper. Then, in tune with the sombre November night, we settle into a discussion that becomes even more glum with more details about Jay's father's hospital. What are the alternatives? What else can or should be done? For a few minutes I brighten. This could turn into a discussion about politics, social priorities. "Maybe it doesn't have to be this way," I offer. Maybe this is the time and the opportunity for us to press hard and demand and design better services for an aging population, a population that will include us before too long. All kinds of things could be done to provide better care. Better care could mean more space, more individual attention. Things could be improved immeasurably by more precise attention even to simple matters such as who is paired with whom in a chronic-care room. My mother has a story of a dear old woman, my Sunday School teacher when I was a child, who spent her last days in fear of being physically attacked by her totally out-of-it roommate. What she needed was to be matched with a gentle soul who still had the wit to discuss African violets. "We're a rich society," I argue. "Whatever is our priority, surely we can make it happen."

For a moment it seems like this topic might have somewhere to go. Then it gets cut short. "We can't afford it," responds my friend, the businessman. "Governments can't be expected to pay for it; the country is broke."

What we will afford, we agree grimly, is death. "The major contribution as the baby boomers age," my friend offers, "might well be a change in the way our society permits death when you no longer want to continue living." Jack Kevorkian, Michigan's "Doctor Death," will be gone by the time we need him to assist in our deaths, but his legacy could be formalized into the kind of system many places in western Europe already have. And as the aged populations get ever larger, this would be broadly appealing because it would be so cost effective. Read: inexpensive. The primary legacy of the baby boomers, as we pass from the scene thirty or forty years from now, might well be making it acceptable for the dying to choose the manner and time of their deaths. Like the Inuit walking out alone onto the frozen tundra at the moment of his choice. Death on demand.

This is pretty depressing. Though Jay is right at least in some small part. We need to face head-on the matter not just of aging, but of death. Including our own. When, how, where, under what circumstances. Within or outside of our control.

Maybe, in the end, the most I can learn on this subject comes, as it should and as it usually does, from my mother. My mother goes to visit old people. Every week she heads off to nursing homes, which are the growth industry of her town, and patiently sits with friends and strangers alike, holding their hands. She indulges their complaints or their confusions. She feeds them their supper. She brushes their hair. She listens. She commiserates with their stories. There is kindness, there is care. The action isn't dramatically heroic. It seeks no medals, it requires no formalized program or heavily debated rationale. It is just something that is done, as in one way or another it has always been done. Seeing someone through to the end of their life is a simple test of humanity.

16

Between Generations

We have children. And then it seems they have disap-peared almost from view. Where did they go? We have parents, and then suddenly they are old people who are happy to be grandparents. And we are the parents. And then the old people are even older and we ourselves are old. And it only took a couple of minutes for this to happen.

People in their forties and fifties are sometimes called "the sandwich generation." Which is kind of an appropriate metaphor, I suspect. Squeezed and turned into egg salad. We are in a certain kind of role with one of the other generations, and we think it will go on forever. Then suddenly it changes. It is over. We think we didn't even have a chance to get used to it. Did we even have a chance to become good at it? What will we do now?

Sarah has her first summer job away from home. For three months my daughter will be a counsellor at a YMCA camp on a beautiful island in a beautiful lake in a beautiful part of the country. She won't be away for the entire four months without a break; every two weeks she gets forty-eight hours off. Six chances to come home. But it costs forty dollars for a round trip bus ticket back to the city. So she has served notice that, unless she can get rides with friends or co-workers, she might not spend her hard-earned cash on the bus every time (the camp is a good experience, but the pay isn't great). Besides, when she does come in, neither her mother nor I stand to see very much of her. There are friends she also won't have seen for twelve full days or longer. And there is more. As well as holding down her first summer job away from home, my daughter has her first serious boyfriend.

What this is really about is the child flying the nest – not just for a summer. Everything is changing, everything is in flux; I am witnessing a major transfer of loyalties, of priorities. From now on, everything will accelerate. She will leave for the requisite year of travel in Europe. She will select a university in another city. She will graduate into a job, a career somewhere probably even farther away. She will get married. She will have her own children.

Sarah is nineteen, almost twenty. It feels like about last

week that she was twelve and we would sit for long sessions on the couch or by her bed late at night trying to work through labyrinthine adolescent insecurities about whether she would be truly and adequately liked by the other grade-seven girls in the school where she was enrolling. The week before that, she was a toddler and we were going to the park to clamber on the swings, the slide, and the big wooden play structure. I felt useful in those days.

Today I pulled a fat file from a little-used cabinet and out spilled a sheaf labelled Sarah's Artwork. The bulk of the drawings and paintings and collages and cutouts date from daycare, when she was four years old. Then they progress along to about grade four, after which things tailed off. It's not that she stopped making art, I just stopped putting it all into the fat folder. In fact, for both the most recent Christmas and the most recent Father's Day gifts, I received beautifully wrought pieces – a small clay sculpture and a papier mâché plate fashioned in studio classes she attends at college. Her plan for next year, when she turns twenty and will be travelling in Europe, is to look through as many of the grand old museums as she can fit in and afford.

But today I took this brief excursion into the past. As I carefully lifted and examined the aging pages, the lump tightened in my throat. The work was silly, clever, beautiful, whimsical, experimental, revealing. Almost every drawing had a solid byline, the stamp of developing identity. Also, there were lots of dedications, "To Dad, Love Sarah," in deliberate, heavy, tongue-out-the-corner-of-the-mouth crayon lines. The drawings leaned heavily to self-portraits and flowers. There were also a number of houses, smoke curling from their chimneys. (Where does this come from? Young children rarely witness smoke curling from chimneys these days, yet that's how they all still draw them.) Among the drawings, too, were short stories, early ones barely legible with even the letters difficult to make out. But then, progress. Here's one written when my daughter was seven:

"One day I saw a worm and the worm was on a stik. So I piked it up and put it in a jar with mud in it. The End."

For me, as it is for most parents, having a child meant I was able to return to my own childhood. At every stage of enjoying my daughter's activities, I would get flashes of my past; sensations more than memories. And those sensations miraculously unlocked doors in my subconscious, doors into rooms long-abandoned and forgotten about. I was able to return to both pleasures and traumas; I could remember once again being unable to sleep before a birthday and I could remember the hurt of not being liked by someone I wanted to be my friend. Having children, I realized, allows one to live life twice (at least). I didn't know this would happen until I went through the experience of being Sarah's father.

When my daughter was three, her mother and I separated. I became one of those dads whose child comes to visit: the bedroom at mom's house, the bedroom at dad's house; two toothbrushes, two sets of pyjamas, two sets of toys. The little suitcase to carry any other things that there weren't two of, between homes. Ours is the generation of the absent father, the separated father, the broken family, the "alternative" family. Those little children did a lot of travelling; they were made of pretty sturdy stuff. Having separated parents was so common it was almost normal; in my daughter's daycare and kindergarten and elementary school, the children from separated families were always in the majority. All manner of arrangements were possible; some had lesbian parents, one had three parents, a few just one parent. In the 1980s, at least in large cities, the separated or divorced family did not carry the stigma it would have in a smaller community or at an earlier time. But there were other things to worry about.

With the phenomenon of family break-up and the culture of divorce came a whole language of terminologies and squabbles and worries. Custody, support, access. Lawyers and complaints. We tried to behave ourselves; the child's best welfare was supposed to be the overriding issue. The matter of adults solving their differences without destroying the lives of their children in the bargain was supposed to be paramount. It was rarely easy. In every case it was a matter of breaking up with a spouse because you no longer wanted to share life together, and then immediately having to put all that hurt and anger behind in order to make wise decisions about continuing together to raise a child or children. People weren't always successful at doing that. Some, often highly educated professional people who you would have thought would know better, did it very badly.

One couple I knew (well, I knew him but never met her) dealt with one another via court order and communicated only through lawyers after they broke up. Their eight-year-old daughter's visits to her father were always sandwiched between telephone calls – his lawyer to her lawyer to her to her lawyer to his lawyer to him. I listened more than once to his litany of anger and humiliation. One Sunday evening I went with him to return his daughter to her mother's house after a visit. Hostilities were at such a level that he needed a witness to confirm that he had returned his child at the agreed-upon hour. I watched the eight-year-old trot up to the front door, which opened only a crack to admit her, looked at my watch, and affixed my signature to my friend's copy of his court order. If there were any arguments later, I would be called on to verify the delivery.

I had my own guilt. For a long time I worried that I had deprived my child of a normal life. A normal life. I wasn't sure what I meant by that. I vaguely thought I meant a life in a house where there were two adults, or at least consistently the same two adults, mom and dad, and maybe the dog. The kind of normal family that television used to have but doesn't any more either. It bothered me a lot. It used to keep me awake at night with worry, both the thought that I was depriving my child of something in the short run, something she should have, and that the deprivation in the long run might have some kind of deleterious effect on her development and her life. She would never be able to love. She would be afraid to be happy.

Then, one day, I decided that was all hogwash. I was beating myself up for no good reason and I was doing no one a favour – particularly not my daughter. I realized that there is no such thing as normal. There is no normal life, there is only the life you have. It can be bad, it can be good. You can be loved and supported and nurtured and nourished and encouraged. Or you can suffer the opposite of all of those. But some objective standard of normal has absolutely nothing to do with it. Or with anything.

New studies now try to tell us that hardly any of it matters anyhow. Behavioural geneticists, who are the flavour of the month on the child-development front, say that once their genetic influences are accounted for, parents have relatively little effect on how children turn out. We, and all the ancestors that have gone before us, bequeath to our children a genetic pattern that is critically important. But that's pretty much the end of our work. Whether the child is going to be outgoing and confident, courageous and able, or by contrast troubled or unhappy, is already ordained in the gene combinations, we're told. Any amount of external influence won't do much to change it. Genes even create environmental factors, suggest the researchers, in that a child who is innately happy will always elicit more positive responses from the people she encounters than the responses elicited by someone who is perpetually sour. A child, therefore, can end up living life in a different environment from even a sibling. The gestures of parents seem peripheral at best. If highly literate parents surround a genetically bookish child with a decent library, the scientists call it a "goodness of fit." If the parents are bookish but the child has genes that are not, the library is just going to be an irritation.

To me these theories seem to get a lot of bad parents off the hook and must make a lot of very good parents frustrated. Because I think there are such things as good parents and bad parents. And I've seen lots of cases where children who may have had very good genes were still damaged by abusive or unsupportive environments. But then, I'm not an expert.

In the parenting theories, the father takes an additional whack. Margaret Mead remarked that in human histories the link between father and child was a late development. Human fatherhood, as we understand it, could be a mere social invention. Even James Joyce labelled paternity a possible legal fiction. Yet maybe it doesn't matter, because in the end what I will cherish about my time with my daughter is not so much what I might have been able to give to her because of our biological connection, but our relationship as two humans and what she brought to my life.

Now I come back to the present. My child is still my child but she is no longer a child. And a great deal is about to change. In the future my role will be to send her money. She will talk to me via long-distance telephone; we will communicate through e-mail. What does all of that mean? What is in store now? I re-experienced my childhood while she was going through hers. Will her adulthood give me some perspective on my life as an adult? How to be a father when your child is in her twenties? This is unmapped territory and scares the dickens out of me. I don't think my job is finished – certainly our relationship is not finished. But what will it look like? Of what use can I be to her?

Her mother and I seem to have muddled through Sarah's teenage years okay. At least one writer on developmental psychology makes a large issue out of the fact that it is not parents but peers who are important in anyone's development. Indeed. But I still know that the push and pull between a person and his or her family goes on for a long time and can do a heck of a lot to make one's life easy or difficult, fulfilled or frustrated. Why else would it be important to rebel as part of growing up? We prepared ourselves and even secretly wished for Sarah's adolescent rebellion. Secretly, because it is a contradiction in terms to design your child's rebellion. We also understood that teenage rebellion only works when it attacks that which is most sacred to you; they need to really hurt you in order to properly declare independence. We tried to be prepared and kept saying, like a mantra, that the wise parent will understand this no matter how hurt they are. In the old wisdom, part of which I still believe, parents drive their children to drug use, suicide, damaging sexual relationships through their own defensiveness and through mishandling the child's natural rebellion.

We waited; not much happened. Friends complimented us on having such a mature, well-adjusted kid. Other people's children were running off to California and bringing home crack addicts to Thanksgiving dinner. Did we miss something? I hope not. There has to be some declaration of independence. Was there enough in our daughter's case? Did we pass the test? I hope so, because I know that the rejection by child of parent that doesn't happen until the twenties and thirties is different than that of the teenage years. More serious. If your child is estranged in her twenties and thirties, then you really have something to worry about.

So here I am watching my child move into the adult stage of her life, not knowing quite what role I ought to have. Will I do a good job? How can I know? These are uncharted waters. But then, the first nineteen years were also uncharted waters.

17

Mortality

Quite often, people who mean well will inquire of me whether I ever ask myself, in the face of my diseases, "Why me?" I never do. If I ask "Why me?" as I am assaulted by heart disease and AIDS, I must ask "Why me?" about my blessings, and question my right to enjoy them. The morning after I won Wimbledon in 1975, I should have asked "Why me?" and doubted that I deserved the victory. If I don't ask "Why me?" after my victories, I cannot ask "Why me?" after my setbacks and disasters. I also do not waste time pleading with God to make me well. I was brought up to believe that prayer was not to be invoked to ask God for things for oneself or even for others. Rather, prayer is a medium through which I ask God to show me God's will, and to give me strength to carry out that will.

— ARTHUR ASHE, *Days of Grace*

Stuart got his prostate scare when he was forty-four. He had taken a new job, and he and his wife and family were getting ready to move halfway across the country. The impending change, for all of them, was terribly exciting. But before Stuart could take his new high-level position in a government legal office, he had to go through the requisite physical.

Whammo.

"Have you heard that Stu has cancer?" my friend Liz asked when the phone chain that started ringing around town reached me.

Blessedly, the diagnosis came early in the progress of his disease, and after emergency surgery the doctors pronounced him cured. But the incident alerted all of us, his friends and, I suspect, his enemies, that henceforth, urologists were going to be our best friends.

Later that summer we sat together on beach chairs staring out at a sun-blazed August lake. Stuart looked remarkably well, though walking required care and peeing remained a major discomfort. Though the doctors had said it would probably be okay, full sexual functioning was a wait-and-see matter. But Stu was changed; I could tell just by the way he squinted at the horizon and talked about his children. Life would never again be looked at or thought about in the ways it had been previously.

The first stark reminder of my mortality arrived when I was forty-three. It also had to do with my dick. It would take a full book to explain, with any exactitude, the precise nature of my rather exotic medical condition, so I will be coy. In brief, I was diagnosed with a rare skin condition on a sensitive part of my anatomy, which the docs charmingly explained as "pre-cancerous." That's terminology designed to put the mind at rest! I was devastated on two counts: first, the use of the C-word (albeit conditionally, with the prefix). And second, because of the part of my body singled out for attack. This was not, I was assured, the price of some careless or foolish (or bad) behaviour; in a perverse way, that would have been preferable because then I could have blamed someone, if only myself. But this skin condition was attributable perhaps to genes, perhaps to chromosomes, perhaps to time. This latter was the worst to contemplate; I was getting old. Things were beyond my control. My body was giving out, betraying me. And the part that was betraying me was a part critically necessary to my notion of myself as a man, a vital man, a desirable man, a functioning man. The blow was awful.

The offending part was a bit of skin about a quarter the size of the nail of my baby finger. If it had been on my elbow or my knee, the term "pre-C" would have worried me, but it would have been a much smaller blow than the one I was experiencing because of its location in that more sensitive, more charged place.

What would I do? All kinds of problems were raised in my mind and in my life. I didn't want to die! I had a child; I had work; I had things I wanted to do. Thoughts about death or its possibility had been only abstract up until then. I liked it that way. I wasn't afraid of death, but I certainly didn't want it soon.

Then I had a period of another sort of panic about my life. I was single, very single. Suddenly I wished I weren't; I wished I had somebody who cared about me, somebody I could trust, somebody who loved me enough that this infirmity wouldn't get in the way. I dreaded what I would have to go through because I was single, still supposedly in the hunt. What explanations would have to be made now whenever I met and got to know a new woman? I considered passing the rest of my life as a celibate.

And then I denied all that. I turned to a rabid twentieth-century faith in my doctors and medical science, which is itself a kind of denial. I would enter the program agreed upon by Allan the urologist and Michael the dermatologist. I trusted them: they had framed, Latin-inscribed certificates from Harvard and Michigan and Toronto and the University of California on their office walls. We would use chemicals to zap this. Two weeks to destroy it, I thought to myself, two more weeks to heal, and I would be good as new. I would be who I was before. The medical magic would work quickly; I could ask out the attractive woman I'd just met, and by the time we reached the stage I fancied we'd reach, there wouldn't even be anything to explain.

Not so. Two years later I was still not clear of it. "This is stubborn," Allan said. After this, life and attitude changed.

This was chronic, which was both good and bad. I couldn't zap it, but I learned I could live with it. It would go away, it would come back. When it came back, I would treat it, control it. I didn't want it to move from pre-C to C, but so far it hadn't. Otherwise, I could live my life. I quickly found I could, with little problem, continue having sex. I developed a tidy, brief explanation to use when necessary and then found that the women I was dating, who by now were pushing middle-age themselves, had their own tales, which they were more comfortable telling to me now that I was also, shall we say, compromised. War stories. You're a gimp, but so am I. What a coincidence! Actually, it didn't seem to matter.

Another realization: a chronic condition makes our weaknesses fully a part of our lives. Our decline is our reality. We are forced not only to acknowledge and live with it, but it becomes our identity. Our endurance becomes our strength. Rather than a burden, it becomes one of the things that we actually like about ourselves, one of the things we're grateful for and celebrate.

This episode wasn't, for me, the end of the world. But it was a big change in my world. And it heralded an even bigger change, the time when the body lets us know – piece by piece, bit by bit – it's going to quit, shut down, change, and eventually die. Thereafter, my body was going to give, one after another, all kinds of other signs of its caving in, signs I would have to respond and adjust to both practically and, more important, psychologically. It would soon be eyeglasses for reading. Then what? Root canals to repair old fillings, laser treatment for the carpal tunnel injury to my left wrist. My body was wearing out. I might look after it – go to the gym, try to eat right, and kid myself that I was in better shape than I had been since I was twenty – but the signs were inexorable. I had a lot of miles on, and sooner or later all parts were going to show wear and require maintenance and regular repair. And then it would only get worse. This was but the beginning.

When we're young, it's not that we think we'll live forever; it's that we don't think about it at all. Death, mortality, chronic health problems, the ticking of the clock are abstract considerations at best. Theoreticals. Midlife is the time when, almost without exception, these former abstractions find ways to wham home in dramatic fashion. And our lives will never again be the same. Confronting our mortality, and everything that implies – weaknesses, limitations, finiteness – is one of the most profound (and most lonely and frightening) passages we will go through.

The confrontation has its way of making us behave differently. We may get foolish. The Olivia Dukakis character in the 1980s movie *Paper Moon*, when asked why her middle-aged husband would slip away from his family to pursue an affair, answers simply: "Fear of death." Almost all of us, at least briefly, do some or all of the requisite things to improve our odds, such as change our eating and exercise habits. We join gyms. We start regimens of running or yoga or tai chi. These may herald permanent lifestyle changes, which can open doors to new experiences and well-being. Or they may be gestures that fall away in short order. A lot of us seek the quick fix of chemicals or pharmaceuticals. Today we have Viagra, and in the last week I've come across three different articles about hormone-replacement therapy, testosterone pills, for men who are going through something called their "andropause." What is interesting are the observations of a number of doctors quoted in the articles, who point out that the pharmaceutical approach is frequently taken by men as a substitute for changing their lifestyles. Drinking less, quitting smoking, getting on a sensible exercise regimen, paying attention to eating habits and stress would improve our lives dramatically. But if a drug or a testosterone cocktail is available, we believe we can use that and keep on behaving otherwise just as before. The other interesting observation is that both Viagra and testosterone treatments target the sexual man. Our penis remains the touchstone, not only of our physical self, but also of our identity and psychological well-being.

But there are no two ways around it – a hair transplant, a face lift, an exercise regimen, a prescription for Viagra, an affair, a red convertible – we still know we are going to die. Though first we are going to get old. This realization increasingly preoccupies us. The life expectancy of a man in North America is now seventy-three years, so we forty-something men have at least two and three decades yet to get old while preparing for the end. And it might be much longer than that; the fastest growing demographic group in America are people over ninety. But the corner has been turned. From now on, no matter how long it takes, our aging, rather than our youth, will more and more absorb us. This is galling and difficult, all the more so for people of my generation who've spent all our lives, thus far, creating and celebrating a culture of youth and youthfulness.

There are perhaps two reasons why every time I pull open a magazine or newspaper I encounter an article about aging. One is that I am, at least subconsciously, looking for them. The topic has become my preoccupation. The second is that more of them are printed. I am a baby boomer. We baby boomers – people born between 1947 and 1966 – are the demographic spike, thirty-three per cent of the total population. We move like a plump bubble across the radar screen of our times. Because of our numbers, we have been and still are the most self-indulgent and self-absorbed generation possibly in the history of the world. What we care about, be it rock and roll, jobs, children, or holiday destinations, gets presented as if everybody should care about it. Our priorities become the political priorities of the day (pity our children). Now we care about getting older. As we care about our retirements, our pensions, our mortality, and the aging and health process, we're bound to hear a lot more about them. David K. Foot, the author of the 1996 bestselling book on demographics, *Boom, Bust and Echo*, pointed out that smart business decisions ought to take the aging population into consideration. We could get rich putting our money into the aging industry: pharmaceuticals, eyeglasses, personal-care homes, and, ultimately, funeral services. (We might also get rich, it seems to me, by investing in the denial industries like cosmetic-surgery clinics and the makers of home exercise machines that will rarely get used.)

We think we want to live forever, but really we don't. It would only be fun to live forever if our body stayed somewhere between twenty-five and forty, and our mind and wits stayed there, too. And also if our friends stayed there on top of their games right with us. I know elderly people, eighty and ninety, who are perfectly healthy in body and mind, but what is life for them when all their friends are gone? Even in your forties, it is no fun watching your friends and contemporaries enter their declines. My friends, one by one, are undergoing knee surgery, cholesterol-control diets, treatments for cancer. The bravest is Jake, my long-time colleague and buddy, who has had both hips replaced. This is an increasingly common procedure, to replace your ball sockets with artificial ones made from space-age materials when the originals, for whatever reason, wear out. The operation, however, has to rip through some of the toughest muscle fibre the body possesses, and leaves you with a lengthy convalescence that starts off with days, even weeks, of excruciating, life-deforming, sleep-killing pain. "But think of the bright side," Jake says. "At any other time in history they wouldn't have been able to do this, and I'd have been consigned to a wheel-chair. I'm buying perhaps another twenty years of walking-around time, even if I am going to be a little stiff."

Of my friends' declines, Jake's may be the most poignant, and his response the bravest, but the worst happened to a fellow who for a while was my lawyer. Until he had his break-down. At age forty-two, he simply didn't show up at the office one day. Within a month, his practice had collapsed. Whispers floated around town about his condition, things that had happened, where he might be now, when or whether he might be back. Rumours had him in California and Mexico. A caretaker took over his law office and eventually we all had our files transferred to other attorneys. He slipped from our minds. Then, after a passage of several years, I was walking down the street one day, and from the other direction approached a shabby figure badly in need of a haircut, a shave, and some clean clothes. He had a contorted, foot-dragging walk, which might have been caused by his trying to keep his feet inside floppy sneakers that had no laces. I did a double-take as he passed. He didn't look at me at all; possibly he didn't know who he himself was, let alone who I was. Good God, I thought.

Do we think differently after we have been brought up short and reminded we are mortal? The answer, unequivocally, is yes. We start to snipe about how youth is wasted on the young after we're forty, when we face the fact that we won't live forever; when we start to realize that being alive isn't always going to be fun. How long ago, then, seems the time when we were beautiful and healthy, when we didn't have to think about cholesterol, when the next erection would be only twenty minutes away, when we could drink all night and still show up for work the next morning, when exercise wasn't a job, and doctors were seen only in emergency rooms.

Predictably, our first response to our new discovery is to scream and rebel. Can't our expensive, shiny medical system do something? It can, of course, and it does. A great deal. Which makes us different from the villager in Zimbabwe who told me he neither worried about nor took precautions against getting AIDS. His reasoning was that even though HIV raged through about twenty per cent of the population in southern Africa, before it got around to killing him he might well die in a war, a fight, an accident, from hunger, or any of a long list of other deadly diseases, which he listed off. So why worry? For us in the West, our prospects are vastly different. Ours is the only time and place, virtually in the history of the world, where we believe we have a right to live, if not forever, then at least to our full, long, ancient old age. From Dr. Spock onward, we have been indulged in a conviction of our preciousness. Ours is the first generation in all of time to feel we're entitled to our full quota of life, and if we don't get it, there should be someone we can sue. Our first instinct, when reminded of our mortality, is to picket in protest.

But eventually we calm down. And then we face another choice, one that has to do not with our bodies but with our spirits. Does our new knowledge change the things we believe and the ways we behave? Do we start the search for centres of spirituality long ignored or perhaps never possessed? Do we stay on side with Dylan Thomas, and know that we inevitably will "not go gentle into that good night . . . [but] rage, rage against the dying of the light"? Or do we search for the sort of spiritual centre that might provide the grace afforded to a man like Arthur Ashe, whom I quoted at the outset of this chapter.

Stuart is fine. He's enjoying life in his new community. He's excelling in his job. His career is thriving. I even saw him on television not long ago, when a comment from his part of the country was required on a substantial matter of public issue. He looked fit, articulate, energetic, still boyishly handsome. But I know a couple of other things, things that put a bit of an edge on everything. Things that betray a mellowing that to me can only be explained in one way. Stuart has become very tender toward his wife, the wife of his second marriage. Just as his big brood of children and stepchildren from two marriages is starting to leave home and spread out across the continent, he has become more attentive and eager to be connected with each of their lives. He keeps up assiduously with friends through e-mail and phone calls, and lunches when passing through town. He is shoe-horning into his busy life another long-restrained passion: he is writing a book, a novel, and his need to write makes him get up early and stay up late to get it all in. He keeps smiling. He keeps one eye on the clock. He keeps attuned to his body. He can never take anything for granted. Ever again.

18

Going to the AIDS Memorial with Neil

In 1993, whoever inscribes the names on the AIDS memorial in Cawthra Park in the middle of Toronto's gay district switched to a smaller size for the lettering. The memorial's custodians, dismayed as the numbers continued to rise, worried they might otherwise run out of room in their confined downtown park, where fourteen discreet concrete pillars form this most poignant of commemoratives. From that year on, each stainless-steel plaque shows seventy-six names in two columns instead of one column of twenty-five names, and you almost need glasses to read them. This is a memorial, with parallels to other memorials. But it is also the record of a storm that has come in and blown its way through a community, as well as across countries and across the world. For 1982, there is only one name on the memorial, a Leland Richards. For 1983, there are twelve. For 1990, there are 160 memorialized deaths. It's said that because of behaviour changes and drug therapies, the numbers of HIV infections are decreasing throughout North America and in western Europe, and this might be reflected here. 1997 has only fifty-eight names. That fact notwithstanding, there are a lot of names on those pillars in the middle of Toronto.

Dale DeMarsh's name is on the list, one of 292 who died in Toronto in 1995. He had been sick since 1989. Six years diagnosed with HIV and suffering the symptoms of AIDS placed him among the longest survivors. I watched him suffer; every time I came to visit, his body was a little more frail, a little more ravaged, his face gaunt and hollow. Dale's was one of those truly ennobling stories; his spirit was so strong it kept him going longer than his body should have. Dale deserved the old and dignified observation, "Nothing so marked his life as the leaving of it." But then in April, when spring was stirring and the buds, after a long winter, were beginning to open on the trees, he died.

Dale was the friend, lover, partner, cohabitant of a long-time friend of mine, Neil. I have known Neil for more than twenty years. I knew him before I thought very much about whether he was gay or not. We worked together on a project when we both lived in Winnipeg, and after he moved away to Toronto, years before I did, we stayed in touch.

When I travelled to Toronto before finally moving there

myself, I would sometimes stay with Neil and Dale and Dale's son Stephen. They referred to their midtown apartment as "the hotel," and there was always room on the couch. If the place were too crowded, I'd escape to a real hotel – they knew so many people from all over the world, there would often be who-knows-who staying there as well. Once, Neil's ex-wife, who worked in South America as a foreign-aid and human-rights worker, used one end of the sectional sofa while I curled up on the other. "This is slightly absurd," I remember thinking. "Here I am sleeping with Neil's ex-wife while he sleeps with his man friend in the next room."

And it was over these years that Dale became ill and died. Though Neil, miraculously, did not.

There is something about homosexuality that catches the rest of us men unprepared. Gay men pose a conundrum for the vast lot of the rest of us. Particularly in modern times, which are not like boy-obsessed ancient Greece, or any number of anthropologically-primitive-yet-sexually-inventive societies, or even nineteenth-century England, where the contours of erotic interest had considerably more elasticity. It has little to do with how sensitive or liberal, politically correct or broad-minded we might or might not be. We are all affected. There is, because of the very existence of this sexual alternative, a kind of subversion; the subversion that a subculture always throws back at its predominant sibling. A mirror is held up. Questions are opened. Do we exist as opposites, or are we at various places along a continuum? There is an element of threat, even to the most liberal straight man. If we are not sensitive, politically correct, or liberal then our fear or loathing will manifest itself in bad jokes or worse behaviour. But for all straights, there is a deeply rooted, primal consideration that confronts both our sexuality and our view of the world.

The first man I knew definitively to be homosexual was George, who worked as a clerk on a construction site where I, then a student, was also employed. I knew George was homosexual because he said that he was, and everyone – all the camp's employees were men – knew it too. Later on, three or four people I'd known as close friends when we were in high school announced that they were gay.

A couple of others I might have suspected, should I have gone so far as to speculate. Strange to say, neither I nor other friends did (which was perhaps to our credit). Remember that in those not-so-long-ago times, to be different risked a much higher cost than is the case today. My recollection is that these fellows may have had giveaway mannerisms (stereotyping in my adolescent days was pretty much limited to the notion of an exaggerated limp wrist or a lisp). But again, I recall these things only in the kind of retrospect that allows you to think back and say, "a-ha!" By and large, we were incapable of articulating our observations. Or perhaps, as adolescents, we were too self-obsessed to truly notice much that was significant about other people.

These friends were popular with the girls, so much so that others of us envied them their ease in female company. But then, when we were in our early twenties, they started announcing. David from my church youth group, Donald from high school, and Warren, who was my friend and lived in the room next door in our dorm during our freshman year at university. And again, with the ring of recognizing something I should have already known, I said, "a-ha!" But what did that mean? It meant we were on different roads. It meant they had always been on a different road. It meant that in the tumultuous sorting-out of identity and sexuality and even aesthetics that bedevils adolescence, they were on a course that was different from mine. What was the same between us was important, but the difference was too substantial to ignore. It meant that even though simultaneously we were growing into men, a huge part of all our future existence would be different. It meant they knew something I didn't, and that in itself was intriguing. The chief categories of social being are race, class, and gender. Gender now carried an added dimension.

From a simple sexual standpoint I cannot imagine being homosexual. Other men are not what turn me on. But even if they did, I would not want to be homosexual within this culture simply because of how difficult such a life must be, even under the best of circumstances. The first problem is the very high risk of being a pariah in one's family. And if not there, then in one's community. That is not something I could deliberately choose; life is hard enough already. So I consider men who are openly gay, who are out of the closet, to be, first off, extraordinarily brave. I have the utmost sympathy for the difficulties of their lives – of both those who are out, and those who face another (greater?) torment because they do not have the wherewithal to be out.

Since I moved to Toronto, I encounter a lot of gay men, in part because the place I live is on the edge of what is locally called the "gay ghetto," a neighbourhood just off one of the city's major commercial and retail intersections. To a new arrival like me, this is in every sense an ethnic neighbourhood. It might be the Italian neighbourhood, the Polish neighbourhood, the Chinese neighbourhood, the Sikh neighbourhood. But instead it is the gay neighbourhood. I feel as I might were I on the edge of Chinatown, or among the Jamaicans or Greeks or Portuguese or Jews or Iranians in their enclaves. I am an outsider. My choice of neighbourhood was not deliberate, but it was also not un-deliberate. It is in the centre of town, which is convenient. And I've always liked to be in the middle of something exotic. Around me in festive variety, in converted Victorian houses and mundane functional storefronts, are busy gay shops and gay bars and gay restaurants, as well as the Gay and Lesbian Community Centre. The Second Cup coffee shop with all the men lounging on the steps out front is a gay hangout, as is the nearby Baskin Robbins ice-cream outlet. The superintendent in my building, a crusty Nova Scotian who at another time might have been called a Bluenose, tells people I'm "the straight fellow." In other words, I'm exotic. On the streets of my neighbourhood, men hold hands, kiss, and display the kinds of affection that, everywhere else, our culture strictly reserves for men with women. You will not see the Polish flag or the Greek flag flying from the balconies of apartments, but the rainbow flag of the international gay and lesbian movement. Purple, blue, green, yellow, orange, red. In the building elevator, men hold the leashes of strange little animals that in any other locale would not quite qualify as dogs.

But pervading all (and influencing all) is the black shadow of AIDS. A stunning fist to the face, a brutal assault. Gay friends have told me that gay culture would not probably have coalesced so dramatically without AIDS. It took, perhaps, such an assault, such a catastrophe, to make people understand what they had together. People who had been shunted to the margins by society's and the family-values culture's disdain for their orientation, people who had often accepted the admonition to live with shame, saw everything differently because of the new urgency. A plague that was so unfair and seemed to target them so exclusively brought in its wake a kind of angry determination. It made people understand other truths: life is important, so it's worth putting up a fight for your rights and the freedom to be yourself; life is fragile and sometimes short, so it's important to celebrate.

Celebrate they do. One weekend in June, heterosexual me found myself in the thick of something called Gay Pride Day. All week, the streets of my neighbourhood had been buzzing, and by the weekend they were sectioned off to accommodate the second-largest gay parade in North America, next to San Francisco's. Seven hundred thousand people, the newspapers said. It had the feel of a feast day, a Bacchanalian revel. A revel of presumption that didn't always go easy on the sensibilities of the "other society."

On Sunday afternoon, hearing the roar of things all the way up in my apartment, I ventured down to be a proper spectator. The crowd – five deep along the sidewalk, as well as clinging to rooftops and window ledges – had a percussion-driven throb. In large part it came from the music on the passing floats, floats pulled on flatbed semis by growling Mack tractors and loaded with balloons and waving drag queens. Between the floats marched all manner of purposeful, politicized people carrying signs: "Parents Supporting Gays," "Children Supporting Gays," "Friends and Neighbours of Gays," "Lesbian Council of Buffalo, New York."

A lusty cheer. The mayor of Toronto rode by on an antique fire truck, waving both arms like an idiot. In the newspapers he declared he would lose votes if he did this, but he was going to do it anyway. It's still early in his term.

The members of a couple of gyms marched by, followed by the Gay United Church under an identifying banner; a toothy pink-smocked pastor blew kisses to the crowd. The church's ranks were made up of a few young men and a phalanx of determined looking older men and women, the type you can always count on (thank God) to fight for liberal causes. Immediately after them came a flatbed truck loaded with spangle-splattered muscle boys in skimpy Calvin Klein underwear, wiggling to the strains of "YMCA." The truck was sponsored by a major brewery. Then came the ethnic contingents, or contingents that heralded gays of colour. African gays (contrary to the emphatic assertion of a young Kenyan I once met who told me that the only gays in his country were visiting tourists) and Asian gays (a few bewildered looking students and a Chinese girl who had shed her shirt). Then, in sequence, came a marching band from the leather fraternity and a bunch of transvestites, including a Marilyn Monroe so well done up that for a moment I was almost taken in. A tall boy festooned with a necklace of feathers, a spectator standing directly in front of me in the crowd, commenced kissing the neck of the man whose hand he was holding.

The power of a plague to bring survivors together might have united and solidified the gay community. But it has also saddened it. It's impossible for anyone who has not been in the middle of a war or a holocaust or some other such calamity to come close to appreciating the stunned sadness a stricken community is capable of experiencing. I go with Neil to visit the memorial. It is November 30, the eve of International AIDS Day. He walks me along, threading through the pillars that stand rigid like stone soldiers, and points out the names of men he knew. Men he counselled at a gay centre. Men who were on that centre's board of directors. Men he knew professionally. Men he played bridge with. Men he loved. He loved Dale; they lived together for thirteen years. A few months before Dale died, they had an anniversary party to which they invited hordes of friends. The food was prepared by Dale's son, then just graduated from chef school.

We find Dale's name and dates of birth and death. He was the same age as I. He worked as a manager in the government office where they issue birth certificates and maintain other important data. His favourite stories were about the people who'd come into his office needing to alter their documents because they'd had sex-change operations. Dale liked to go to the symphony. He liked to go to football games and watch them on TV. He liked to travel. Before he became sick he talked a lot about his impatience to reach retirement age so he could indulge all those pleasures, especially the travel. He never got to retire.

Neither did most of the others whose names and dates are etched into the cold steel plaques. I look at the memorial; the average age of everyone listed is thirty-eight or forty.

A few years ago, Neil asked me to write a contribution for a book his community was publishing. It was to be called *A Family Portrait*. At that time, gays were engaged in a strenuous battle on numerous fronts to get recognized by officialdom, by things like insurance schemes, pension plans, and adoption laws. Gay couples wanted to be called "families" in order to obtain the same legal and financial rights possessed by people who lived with heterosexual spouses. They were also trying to find social comfort by making use of a term that for such a long time had excluded them. None of it was going to be easy. Their foes were fighting a tenacious rearguard action against both legal and social redefinitions. And at the other end of things, definitions were expanding so rapidly, somebody quipped that a family could be "any four people seen together on *Donahue*."

Neil wrote in his introduction, "Families are obviously defined in many ways, especially for us in the gay community. They include friends, relatives, lovers, and those important to us. We speak of them as our family."

Then I had to decide what I would write, what I might contribute. By writing a contribution to Neil's book, I would be somehow de facto adopted into his family, joining his older sister, a niece, Dale, and Dale's son, Stephen. This would be a little bit of social subversion, which was okay with me. Here's some of what I wrote:

I never think of Neil as a "gay friend." He is always just a "friend." Neil was really the first friend I knew who was gay; who said he was gay. I have had friends over the years who I suspected, no, I guess I knew were gay. But that was in the late 1960s and 1970s and they, for their reasons, weren't saying anything. And I, too polite or lacking the words, said nothing either. But Neil announced it. He told me as he told others. And what that did, I'll always believe, was make me come out of my own closet. We have closets too, we straights. We must be provoked, at least the first time, to acknowledge the gayness of a friend, so we can then both get on with the friendship.

Identity, someone has said, is discovered through our use of mirrors. There is no self without others. So who am I that I would not have been without Neil, without Dale, without George or Donald or David or Warren or any of the rest of the gay men who've been important friends over the years? Who is the me that I see in the mirror of these men? Without AIDS would my view be different? My view of them, even my view of myself? What I see in the mirror is not just my different sexuality, but a man who has been spared a host of other problems and difficulties, from name-calling as a boy to being shunned by family and former friends, job discrimination, political prejudice, and ultimately a front-line confrontation with a devastating plague. I feel spared and safe. Do I feel lucky? Do I think about it at all?

19

Super Bowl Sunday

The typical football viewer is a guy who's had his ass chewed off at the office, who's figuring out how to afford another baby, whose wife just presented him with three overdue bills, and whose teenager busted up the car and then sulked all week. Now he wants to forget all that. He wants to sit back and enjoy the sheer beauty of a perfectly delivered pass or watch a linebacker stomping someone the way he'd like to stomp his boss.

— FRANK GIFFORD, FORMER FOOTBALL GREAT AND COMMENTATOR ON ABC'S *Monday Night Football*, IN HIS AUTOBIOGRAPHY

Man cannot escape being born of woman, but he can, and if he is wise will, as soon as he comes to manhood, perform ceremonies of riddance and purgation.

— JANE HARRISON, *Themis, a Study of the Social Origins of Greek Religion*

 My friend Damien, spending his first winter in North America, thought I was joking when I told him he would see people in the crowd wearing yellow wedges of cheese on their heads. Damien should have known better; he has lived in England, where football fans are certainly every bit as boisterous and bizarre as any in North America. And when it comes to fan violence – what the English call hooliganism – they are infinitely worse. Coming out of Wembley Stadium, you can expect to be assaulted. In America, sports fans, including the cheesehead partisans of the Green Bay Packers, are mostly just ridiculous.

We weren't, by the way, in the stadium. We were in my friend Ian's living room; the game would be on TV, broadcast from far-away San Diego or Pasadena or someplace with palm trees and mid-January sunshine. Outside *our* windows, winter plodded on, grey and cold.

We were clutching frosty bottles of beer and looking at big bowls of potato chips, acutely aware that we had a duty. And that was to engage in an important ritual of bonding. This bonding would take place with one another, and with whichever of Ian's friends might call or stop by during the course of the afternoon. But more than that, we were about to share a number of hours of intense focus which supposedly would unite us with men all over North America – even the world. Super Bowl Sunday is one of the most extensive male-bonding festivals in our culture. Should we ignore it, it would be like missing Christmas. We'd deserve the emptiness we'd inevitably feel. We'd deserve any resulting ostracism from friends or co-workers. And we'd deserve the feeling of solitariness, the dread that we might never *really* be part of anything.

For those reasons, we entertained no thought of letting down the side. We intended to do our job, which was to be guys. And part of that job was to introduce this friend from England to one of the rituals on this side of the Atlantic. This shouldn't have seemed beyond do-able; they not only have sports in England, they have public schools. England, surely, is the home of male-bonding rituals.

Ian, who after a while appeared not to care much about the game, played the perfect host. He fetched more beer. Damien kept diverting us with questions about the unfamiliar game. "Can you explain what they're trying to do now?" he would ask as Brett Favre strode frustrated from the field, and the kicking team came on. He'd ask such questions all afternoon until we realized how impossible it was to explain the intricacies of North American football in one go, especially using as the example such a lavishly interrupted contest as the Super Bowl. Damien's interest, however, was a good sign of the sincerity of his commitment to the larger purpose, which was to bond.

Men have always desired and sought means of bonding. Despite romantic images of loners, men are fundamentally social beings. We may be competitive, but we are essentially co-operative as well. Few of us are strong enough or perverse enough to be truly solitary. Men achieve things, from making war to making movies, through pack coordination. We believe it is the genius of our gender. Take us away from one another, isolate us, and we are lost souls. One of the remarkable stories of our time was Nelson Mandela's triumph over his years of prison isolation and his ability to return, as if from the dead, to be such a co-operative, collaborative leader of South Africa. This doesn't often happen.

Men have also always looked for ways to belong to something larger than themselves. Male ritual has deep roots in an ancient past of struggles, competitions, and fights. Michael Ignatieff, in his 1997 book *The Warrior's Honour*, fears for the end of this and laments the lapsing of the honour-laden warrior culture. "Warrior codes of honour are among the oldest artifacts of human morality," he writes, "from the Christian code of chivalry to the Japanese *bushido*, or 'way of the warrior,' the strict ethical code of the Samurai developed in feudal Japan and codified in the 16th Century." The codes brought men together, systematized their relationships, and told them how to behave. They established rules of conduct and a system of moral etiquette by which warriors – on both or all sides – judged themselves to be worthy of mutual respect. Very broadly mutual: though they might kill one another, if they did so by behaving honourably, even enemies would be "brothers in death." "Without codes of conduct," Ignatieff declares, having a pretty good view of our bloody century, "war is no more than slaughter."

The football players replicate this. Dressed up in their helmets, protective padding, and uniforms – like warriors – they share a code. Their allegiance, however, seems to be more to their calling, football, than to any team or any team's fans. It's hard, I would imagine, to be genuine rivals or enemies when you might be traded to a different club at any moment. We accept the players, with few exceptions, as armies of mercenaries. But like Ignatieff's warriors, they are separated from their civilian watchers. (If nothing else, their contracts do it. Few of us can possibly identify with multi-million-dollar salaries or problems of free agency.)

As in chivalric times, though, the religious, or "Christian," aspect of the code remains intact. The reliance of great numbers of the players on God is pantomimed through elaborate kneel-down displays after a touchdown or even a successful catch. There is something both quaint and mind-boggling about the unabashed insistence of these (mostly) southern (mostly) black young men that God has a role in their game. For example, when asked about two interceptions thrown by Pittsburgh Steeler quarterback Kordell Stewart in an earlier game, Denver Broncos tight end Dwayne Carswell explained, "God could have caused that." Prominent theologians resisted the argument that God would care to intervene in a single football game, but Reggie White, Green Bay Packers defensive star (and a minister with a church in the off-season) rebuked them indignantly: "How do they know? They're not God." We, their audience, watch this partly with disdain and partly with envy, perhaps secretly wishing we could claim the similar support of a war god to help us in our puny battles.

Though billed as a contest, the Super Bowl isn't something that really requires those watching to take sides. Being a partisan, I realized, was largely irrelevant. At the outset of the game I wasn't cheering for either team; I decided to let the spectacle unfold and see where my emotions might settle. In the end there would be a short-lived catharsis for those cheering the winner – Denver this time – but they would share infinitely more with the supporters of the losers than with any man who did not watch the game. What was important was to be adjacent to the experience, close to something larger than themselves. As with a war, those who have been there, on whichever side, know where they have been. The outsiders are those who were never there.

If war, and its later incarnation, team sports, is one model for intense, ritualistic male bonding, another model is the hunt. Equally deeply rooted in our genetic past is the hunter culture. Trust, loyalty, fidelity come through mutual dependence, shared passion, and shared experience. The hunt is another intensely co-operative venture and was especially so when scouts and beaters were required to collaborate rhythmically to drive prey toward the kill. The hunt bound men both to nature and to each other. Today the hunt still has strong roots, though fewer and fewer practitioners. My friend Jake is a hunter who hasn't given it up. He owns five guns, from a Remington 870 Wingmaster shotgun given him by his father when he was a teenager, to a German-made Anschütz

.22 calibre rifle which he is delighted to own simply, he says, because "it's the world's best." Jake was taught to hunt by his dad, and hunting was a critical part of their father-son bond. Every fall now, in part to honour that, he goes out to shoot at ducks and geese on golden October mornings when the flocks are gathering for the great annual migration. Later, when the first snow has fallen, he heads off to try to bag himself a deer.

Like the fishing Jake engages in during spring and summer, hunting is undertaken in order to maintain perspective. Other things in life, business problems, even health matters, can seem transitory when placed against the rhythms of nature and this ancient quest. A man needs something in his life to maintain such perspective, and the ritual of the yearly hunt can do the trick.

But the fishing and hunting quests are also pursued in order to bond. Jake never does these things alone. His duck hunting is always done in the company of another man. His deer hunts are usually undertaken with a group of four or five fellows he has known since high school, men he trusts and with whom he shares a history and a language, right down to their bizarre repertoire of private jokes. The connections are deep and incontrovertible. When Jake told the woman he was dating that, whether or not she was in his life, he would still want to go off duck and deer hunting, she was aghast. She had confused his hunting urge, misinterpreting it as something that could be replaced by his urge for her. It was something, she thought, he was doing out of boredom, to bide his time until something better, more interesting, more civilized, more inclusive of women came along. How wrong she was.

But this male rite is on the wane. Only a small percentage of those who might have done so a generation ago hunt today. The practice is under strenuous attack from many sides, not least among them animal-rights activists and gun-control crusaders. Their attack on hunting argues that it has no place in a crowded, species-depleted world. A battle has been stirred by this. Among hunters, the most passionate still possess enough breath to mount periodic counter-offensives. One, Professor Leon Craig, a political philosopher from the University of Alberta (a school in a region where there's no irony in making the claim that "men are still men"), described attacks on hunters and hunting as attacks on manliness. And worse, Craig declared, such attacks are "a legitimization of the weakness of weak men."

Yet there seems to be trouble in paradise.

The best corporate offices or political parties or trade unions might still be places of natural bonding, but they are now far from being exclusively male. Even the military in most Western countries is going through the process of welcoming women not only into all the ranks, but also into the formerly exclusively male combat units. Most everything that is all-male in our culture smacks of being either contrived or broadly vicarious (and passive).

Contrivance is not really anything new. My uncles belonged to lodges. Every Wednesday night they would put on strange costumes with sashes across their vests, don their fezzes or tricorn hats, and head off to an ornate building in the middle of town known mysteriously as "the lodge." There were many kinds of lodges – Oddfellows, Masons, Optimists, Shriners, Knights of Columbus, Moose, Elk – as well as some more modern and relaxed entities called "service clubs" – Lions, Rotary, Kinsmen. And of course, there was the Legion, where "the war" was relived and refought over and over by men (and some women) for whom it had been the defining, most interesting and exciting, as well as most fearsome, moment of their lives.

Ceremonies, costumes, passwords, hierarchies, rituals, and secret handshakes made these lodges seem awesome places to a nine-year-old, and the uncles enviable characters. Eventually I figured out that the lodges were basically elaborate versions of the treehouse and secret handshake I shared with my friends. The uncles, though, were not nine years old; they were balding and portly. Yet they gave no inkling that what they were doing was stupid or silly. They were totally unselfconscious about the enterprise. The password they had to use to get through the door, the initiation rites to belong to the lodge, were as normal and acceptable to them as the ritual of mowing the lawn. Their wives – my aunts – indulged them. Being inordinately practical and down-to-earth women, they couldn't possibly have taken the lodge ventures seriously. But they didn't laugh, at least not openly, at the uncles. Some of the lodges were so secret and so specific that the aunts or spouses could only go to very prescribed once-a-year parties. The regional or national or international conventions were often men only (except for the hookers who worked the hotels, I later found out). And the rites, the elaborate systems of fantasy, were mind-boggling. One time I saw three Shriners explaining the Middle Eastern basis for their Temple to a bewildered looking Arab student who had happened by one of their parades. The poor lad could only scratch his head and eye suspiciously the baggy pants, fez hats, and scimitar swords sported by these rosy-faced and portly North Americans.

But, like hunting, such clubs are not nearly as important now as they once were. As a teenager I was once taken to give a speech about young people, for which I'd won a prize, to the Thursday-night dinner meeting of our town's Lions Club. Every man who was anybody or who wanted to be anybody in the community was there. The man who owned the Chrysler dealership; the manager of the supermarket; the community recreation director; the mayor; the manager of the bank. Almost all my male high-school teachers were present, decked out in purple vests with buttons and crests sewn all over them. The "tail twister" circled the room, making errant members pay fines for the most ridiculous of reasons. Bad jokes were told. Had we been functioning adults back then, I suppose, my friends and I, everybody I know now, would have had to belong to that group. But as it is, nobody I know of my generation belongs to a service club, much less a fraternal-order lodge.

Why? Are we too selfish to be in a service club? Are we too individualistic to join a group? Are we so thoroughly scattered by our mobile culture and so thoroughly alienated from one another and from our communities that we can't lend our energies to such a collaborative thing? Or do we have something else that fills the hole? Has televised sport filled the gap, imperfectly but yet so very perfectly?

On looking at traditional bonding forms, participation seems to be the important element. With sport, at the end of the day, catharsis happened in the locker room, the all-male preserve. I've heard women speak dismissively about men's "locker-room talk," assuming it is always sexual in content and derisive of women. In my experience it is rarely, if ever, that. Men don't bond by discussing their relationships with or their conquests of women, or even their opinions of women. Men are much more private about those matters. The locker room bonds on another level. But with the specialization of sport, more and more, only the specialists are left to bond there.

Which brings us back to football and the shift from participant to observer and from active to vicarious involvement. Sociologist Dr. Theodore D. Kemper of St. John's University, in the context of an examination of testosterone, speculates about the vicarious dominance experienced by the kind of men who watch sports, in particular football. "This group of males has little opportunity for dominance at work," Kemper says. And so in order to obtain the sense of well-being that can only be provided by a surge of testosterone, they need to find their mode of dominance vicariously. Spectator sport provides this. They get their fix through watching sports and this, he argues, becomes one of the important factors minimizing the likelihood that this huge group of males will ever rebel and challenge the social order. These are the same results the Roman rulers sought when they supplied the masses with bread and circuses. It is working so well that the NFL has been able to negotiate a deal worth $17.6 *billion* for television rights for the next five years of football games.

Super Bowl Sunday proceeds like a day with the Romans at the Coliseum; the Christians loosening up, the lions sharpening their teeth, the crowd buying popcorn. Or a medieval feast day filled with abandon and excess. But, for a number of men I know, something else is underlying the day, something closer to despair. What are we to do now? Something deep inside us wonders how we're going to fill our Sunday afternoons and our Monday nights when the football season ends.

Well, there is hockey and basketball. And in less than three months, baseball will start. But it is nevertheless an unsettling moment. The end of a sports season doesn't create a holiday or a welcome break; it starts a withdrawal from dependency. What has come together in the last couple of decades of the twentieth century is a most powerful bonding, on several levels, between middle-aged men and professional sport.

Some months later, as the hoopla of Wayne Gretzky playing his last hockey game before retirement was unfolding, a female friend remarked, "It's a good thing we have hockey so that men can still be great." She then questioned whether there was anything equivalent for women. But the interesting thing, I thought, was that while she was nodding toward the great gentlemanly role model, Gretzky, his presence in the room came via the television screen. With what actually are we identifying? Author David Denby has characterized modern life as "all about watching without danger." And in another of his prescient moments, three quarters of a century ago, philosopher Bertrand Russell explained that, because modern life is often a life against instinct, many people lead lives that are listless and trivial. As a result, they constantly search for excitement. Our quest is often not for real, but vicarious, experience. A goodly part of men's relationships, even with other men, particularly through something like watching football or hockey on TV, is that of sharing a vicarious experience — at a safe distance. And following that, the bonding of middle-aged men is not so much with each other as it is with our television sets. In the absence of the possibility that sixty million of us North Americans can all be in the stadium at one moment, television — our new community, possibly our real community — has stepped into the breach. Sixty million men sit alone — or, at best, in twos and threes — in our living rooms or dens with our TVs and our remotes (almost a Freudian bit of nomenclature there). Critical to the relationship between a man and his television nowadays is the little chocolate-bar-sized piece of plastic and battery cell that you hold in your hand and use to surf the dial. A friend of mine acknowledges that when he is away from home for any length of time he goes into withdrawal. What Gregg misses when he is away is not his TV, but his remote. His hand feels empty, his thumb twitches. He breaks into cold sweats. He loves his remote; he sits with his ever-widening derrière in his big TV chair, and he is in charge. He doesn't so much watch TV as surf the dial, the ever-expanding sea of channels. It gives him a powerful sense of control, so much so that when he no longer wants to listen to his wife talking at him, he infuriates her by pointing his remote at her in jest and clicking. Super Bowl Sunday is the one day in the year when the remote is barely used; there is nowhere else to go.

Does football (still) matter? When *Esquire* asked this question in an issue with Brett Favre and Peyton Manning on the cover in September 1997, they already had an answer. "It matters," concluded the writer, Charles P. Pierce, "like gravity matters." The problem is that it matters more and more for the wrong reasons. It matters in ways it never did before. It is no longer the bond of the players on the gridiron and the community cheering them on that matters. Football matters deeply now for the community of television, the overriding community we now all share. It is vicarious living of the highest order.

20

Cars and Cigars

[Never] purchase your first sports car in your fifth decade – especially if it's a red one. [Never] get personalized license plates – unless your state will permit tags that read A-S-S-H-O-L-E.

– *Esquire,* D E C E M B E R   1 9 9 9

In early 1998, I sold my car, a white Jeep Cherokee I'd owned for ten years. I'd moved to the middle of Toronto; I lived in a high-rise building. I could walk to the gym, my favourite library, the grocery store, not to mention more than twenty movie screens. Underground parking in my building cost $58 a month and within the first week of living there, my car was burgled. It cost $140 to replace the broken glass and would have cost at least another $450 had I put in a new tape deck. Insurance? My loss about equalled the deductible.

When I was thinking what to do about the matter of my ten-year-old Jeep, my first thought was to replace it. But then I did a financial calculation. Say I bought a $25,000 new car;

whether I paid cash or financed it, the cost in interest paid or lost would be about $1,500 a year. And an automobile, as everyone knows, is not an investment that appreciates in value. After a year, that $25,000 would have a market value of $12,500. If I managed to hang on to it for another nine years, it would be worth . . . nothing. Cost of depreciation: $2,500 a year. By the time I'd added in the licence, insurance, gas, parking, and maintenance, I realized that a new car would cost me at least $6,000 a year. $500 a month. You can ride a lot of subway for $500 a month. You can take a lot of taxis.

Then I undertook a psychological calculation. To not have a car would leave someone like me, who had grown up in the country and learned to drive when I was twelve, feeling a bit naked. I had always had a car; my first automobile was a cream-coloured '66 Volkswagen Beetle, which I bought with summer job money when I was eighteen years old. This might not be easy. But then, I rationalized, maybe it would be good to do something different, something that didn't seem easy. This might push me into a new and different realm; it might prove liberating.

I took the plunge. I took my old Jeep on one last nostalgic drive, cleaned out ten years' worth of whatevers, and removed the plates. Then, in exchange for a $1,200 check, I handed the keys over to a twenty-five-year-old Egyptian man in the east end of Toronto. I went home on the subway.

I felt smug. For the next few days I would step from my building in the morning, my pockets lighter of keys, look at the gnarl of rush-hour traffic, and think *not me!* I walked past cars parked at expired meters, yellow tickets stuck tauntingly under their wiper blades, and I would think, *not me*! I listened to the traffic that hummed well into the night and looked at the air-pollution figures published daily in the newspapers, and I would think, none of this is created by me any more. I walked past the big posted signs for gasoline prices, prices that regularly inched skyward a tenth of a cent at a time, and I would smile to myself.

I wasn't smug for very long. A couple of weeks after selling my car I attended a reception at an art gallery and introduced myself to a smashing red-haired woman. We fell into spirited conversation (just the kind you always hope you'll have), and after a bit of this I asked if she'd like to have dinner sometime. "Certainly," she said. Then she told me where she lived: in Brampton, one of the outer suburbs.

"What do you mean, you don't have a car?" she said.

I still don't have a car. Months have passed, and I have no immediate plan to change my car-less status. Maybe I never will. The red-haired woman and I had one date where she drove in to the city and picked me up, and then one date where I rented a Mercury Topaz and drove out to her jumble of twelve-lane-highway interchanges and suburban condos. Then that was that.

It's almost impossible to describe adequately the nuances of the relationship between men and cars in our culture. It operates on many levels and has roots that go deep, probably to the earlier affiliation between a man and his horse or a man and his team or his carriage. His mode of personal transportation, for some reason, says all kinds of things about a man, and is intricately woven into his psyche and his identity (both public and self). It is an extension of his self, like his clothing. It is a signal of his personality and his person. I remember seeing an article one time in a popular magazine that matched various public figures and celebrities with the brand of automobile they most resembled and the brand they were most likely to be caught driving. The piece was meant to be lighthearted, yet its bite was anything but. It hit the nail square on the head. When they said a certain public figure was a Mercedes convertible, we knew exactly what they meant. That a certain prominent newscaster was a Pontiac also hit the mark.

A car is a means of transport, but it is simultaneously everything else. "Will the future understand," John Updike asked in his book *Self-Consciousness*,

> how much of our lives was spent in automobiles, and how largely their little curved caves of painted metal, speeding through a landscape of imploring advertisements and commercial desolation, and the powerful instant responses of their knobs and pedals, and the fine points of their amenities and costliness, and their aura of controlled explosion were part of our coming of age, our mating, our fulfillment of obligations, our thrusts of dreaming?

Men are interchangeable with their cars, it seems. So we men who don't own cars, what in the world are we?

I won't say that the non-start of anything interesting with the red-headed woman had anything to do in the end with my car-less state. But who really knows? Was I a different man by being a man who had no car (just as I supposedly would have been a different man, in my own mind at least, had I been the owner of a Mercedes as opposed to a Pontiac)? This is overwhelmingly and almost exclusively a male thing, I might add. A prominent woman writer was once asked what kind of car she drove, only to answer, "I think it's a blue one." We men are different. Shallow as it will seem, I believe that my first marriage broke up, in part at least, because I realized that if I stayed married I would never own a four-wheel-drive vehicle, one of those monsters they now call an SUV. I had my eye, in those days, on an International Scout. My wife, quite reasonably, considered that choice totally impractical. But more to the point, she let me know she considered me somewhat deficient for voicing it. This, of course, wasn't the overt cause of the marriage ending, but I believe it was a factor. What had happened was that an identity I thought I wanted to establish was given a signal that it could never emerge under present circumstances. Way back in the deep recess of the male mind, we periodically take stock of what our life is turning into and what it will look like as time passes. And a man's car appears to be a critical part of that bind of identity.

I have still not escaped the connection between cars and men. Attempts to put some spin on it don't work particularly well. Somebody recently praised me – without my car – as "ecologically correct." That should have made me feel good, and did so for about two minutes. But deep down I know that I'm no hero on that scale. Things are easy for me: I no longer have kids to transport to ballet lessons and hockey games; I don't have to get out to some distant ex-urban business park or industrial park to a job; I don't have to stock up on weekly groceries for five. Then again, did I hear it wrong, that comment I thought to be a compliment? Did I miss the sarcasm in that supposedly flattering voice? The paradox in my attitude toward the automobile is a symbol of other deeply conflicted forces and desires that do battle within me. On one level, I long for the security of identity that prevents a man from seeing his car as part of himself. Likewise, I want to be ecologically correct; I despise what the automobile (and our love of it) has done to our cities and our landscape. I hate the use of the automobile as the extension of a penis, which I witness every day when the over-testosteroned young and not-so-young men accelerate their cars up my street. Yet I'm a recovering addict and I can't stand any bullshit. Every once in a while my weakness emerges. I catch myself salivating when I see a nice little BMW convertible idling at a curb. Midnight blue.

One day, I walked into a glassy showroom, like an alcoholic to a tavern. This was one of those premier auto dealers specializing in Audis and Porsches and Saabs; top-of-the-line machines. The room was more like a church than a retail emporium, a lofty construction of steel and glass. I made the point of stopping immediately inside the door to inhale: new rubber, rich leather, cold steel, the most pleasant smells in the world. There were three new Audis – Quatros – on the limited space of the floor, and a silver Porsche Carrera up by the prow window. I looked around. Three men, two of them probably salesmen, the third, a wealthy-looking older gentleman, were huddled next to the more expensive Audis, murmuring discreetly. The younger salesman, an East Indian of about twenty-seven, reached out and gently caressed the car's fender. A dealership for expensive automobiles is night and day from your average edge-of-town Ford showroom; the staff had the haughty obsequiousness of head waiters. I picked up and fondled a glossy brochure. Three other sales representatives worked at desks or on the phone. In a minute, one of them, a young woman in grey pinstripe trousers and jacket, got up and strode over to me. "I'm Adrienne," she said sticking out her hand. She was over six feet tall.

I felt I needed to act like I was interested in everything but not too interested in anything. Adrienne played along, as she no doubt did a dozen times a day. I asked about Saabs, wondering if she would be able to tell that in no way was I the kind of guy who possessed a Saab bank account. She went to her desk and called up some lease information on her screen. When she turned back to face me, my imagination flashed an image of her in shiny thigh-high boots and holding a coiled whip. "I think a Saab 9000 would be just right for you," said Adrienne, eyeing me coolly.

For a few minutes we batted numbers around in the hypothetical way people do when significant sums of money are involved. Adrienne's lease rates seemed a little stratospheric, so I mentioned that I hadn't yet had a chance to look at anything over at the Infiniti dealership on Yorkville, a nearby street of similarly lavish tastes. This elicited a tight smile and the acknowledgement that perhaps she might have another look at what she could offer. We shook hands again and exchanged cards. I left feeling wonderful. Sated somehow, as though I would be good now for another six months.

"Cigars and Corvettes are for advertising, ways of announcing to the world, I can afford these things. I'm a big hunter." – Bill Bryson commenting (in the *Globe and Mail*, July 4, 1998) on the so-called male midlife crisis.

On page 385 of the four-hundred-page December 1998 issue of the monthly magazine *Cigar Aficionado* is a photograph of a "cigar dinner" put on by a group of German and American businessmen. In order to hold the dinner, they rented a section of the Great Wall of China. In came tables and chairs, white linen and silver, and then an army of middle-aged Occidental men with baseball bats in their mouths.

By the time anybody reads this, I hope the cigar craze that obsesses the pseudo-stylish will have abated. At the moment, however, it is still going full tilt. The newsstand where I buy magazines and the weekend papers carries six journals devoted exclusively to cigar smoking. A couple of them are as thick as Sears catalogues. There are features with celebrities like Arnold Schwarzenegger smoking cigars. There are articles about the making of cigars and, of course, the ranking of good, better, and best cigars. There are advertisements telling us how to obtain a "smoking calendar" featuring twelve gorgeous women and, best of all, a "nude cigar smoking video." The concern with seeking public pleasure from these rather gross appendages is huge. If done at all, the enjoyment of a cigar should rather, I think, be a solitary act, or a surprise. One person smoking alone, contemplatively, at an out-of-doors sporting event, say a horse race. Or Dylan Thomas–style uncles on Christmas afternoon. Not twenty guys all puffing away as they surround Claudia Schiffer. But cigars have become, as Bill Bryson points out, advertisements for oneself.

In my late forties, I've entered the silly season of a man's life. In the same way as it's a pity that youth is wasted on the young, it's also too bad that the possession of sometimes scandalous amounts of money is wasted on men my age. But it seems as if one last, loud, braying bit of assertion is needed. And if we have the wherewithal, we make sure our bray is good and loud.

At this time of life it seems we have two urges. One is to strip ourselves bare and become monklike in our simplicity. The other is to load ourselves with all manner of distracting paraphernalia. Sometimes this is where men part ways, each of us choosing one or the other of the paths. Sometimes a conflict exists within one man, a paradox, like the Olympic sprinter who spends thousands of dollars to shave an ounce off the weight of his running shoes but goes into the hundred meter race still loaded down by a gaudy gold chain around his neck. We are unresolved and daily do internal battle; one day smugly comfortable to be free of debt and ecologically correct, the next unable to resist the Saab in the show window.

While I'd be an idiot to decry or deny the pleasures to be derived from a well-crafted car or a well-made cigar, possessing either one is not so much about enjoyment of physical, material goods as it is about other things. Perhaps it's gratification delayed, making up for the toys we failed to get as children, which is something I remember when I was seven years old plotting to do later when I had unlimited finances: buy out the toy store. More likely it has to do with identity. Or proving something. Though if proving something, we don't seem sure exactly to whom.

If we think the right car or cigar is going to get us the attention of women in ways that will do us any good, we're on the wrong track. I've never met a woman who was attracted in a positive way to a cigar. Amusement is as good as it gets. I've never met a wife who thought more of her husband because the curtains in the living room stunk from years of his smoke. I've never met a single woman who got weak-kneed at the sight of a man puffing on a good cigar. Cars are a bit the same. My red-headed friend certainly liked the convenience of my having an automobile in order to pick her up from her remote suburb. Cars for women, though, seem largely to be for only that: convenience, safety, warmth. At some level a good car might represent the ability of the man to be a "provider," but they don't achieve anything at nearly the level we men might like to think.

Likewise, I don't think we're impressing the young or our children. They're too busy with themselves and each other.

Which means we men, in our Bryson-ish "big hunter" guise, are setting out mainly to impress one another. Which forces us to ask, is this necessary? And does it work? To answer the first question, I fear so. Probably not, in answer to the second. At best, it might cause envy (which has been identified as the only one of the deadly sins not to give us any pleasure). Yet something in us needs to do it anyway. At every stage in a man's life there's a mandate for some kind of strut. When he's young, it's an energy that leads to fighting and wars. At forty to fifty, I'm afraid, it leads to expensive cars and lovingly fondled cigars.

21

I've never seen a moose in the territory around Loon Cottage, though I once examined, with a procession of dozens of the curious, a car that had hit a big bull at a curve along Highway 71. It happened in the early morning. The car was a voluminous black Cadillac, and its hood was caved, its windshield smashed, and the front of its roof crunched as if a building had fallen on it. There are definitely moose hereabouts; the Ojibwa at Onigaming and the local hunters manage to pot a few for the freezer every fall. But moose, living at the periphery of the bush and grazing in the marshy shallows at the edges of lakes, like to mind their own business. Unlike deer, or the local bears, who are social animals – and indiscriminate – moose, in their own indubitable opinion, are perhaps too good for any kind of regular ongoing interaction with humans. Inside the great head lies some well of prehistoric wisdom. They are smart as well as shy and cautious; they leave the deer and the bears to integrate.

Black bears are almost ubiquitous throughout North America, except where their habitat has been destroyed or diminished. In the south, this diminishment is happening everywhere. But where there is still bush cover, and places to scamper off and den in for the winter, black bears are plentiful. They are notorious scavengers. In this part of the country they live on blueberries and wild raspberries (which are usually found in abundance) until either they run short of these or discover human garbage. Garbage, both that of travellers along the highway and in the parks, and the private refuse of residents and cottagers, must be kept inside padlocked boxes fortified with thick wire mesh. Otherwise, the bears will be into it. Once a bear gets a taste, he'll never leave you (or your trash) alone. Just as for a tabloid reporter, garbage is a bear's Valhalla. The community garbage dump is the ultimate treat, but it carries a price. Bears who manage to find the big, central municipal garbage dump descend into a total moral spiral, never again having an honourable life. In the end, they have to be shot, or tranquilized and transported.

Black bears, however, are rarely dangerous. They are not like grizzlies or polar bears, aggressive by nature and keeping humans justifiably wary and fearful. Black bears are mainly just a nuisance. Our fears and prejudices, rooted in too many childhood stories, are a great disservice to them. And it turns out to be a practical disservice as well; our fear of bears seems to get a lot of them killed, I would say unnecessarily.

My appreciation of nature is that of a twentieth-century urban man. At the high end, I hope. That is, I don't know anything but wish I did. I'm a step beyond a romantic, yet nowhere near expert. I escaped, and tried to protect my child too, from enmeshment in the Disney-style anthropomorphism of wildlife. But I struggle to maintain a view of the world that keeps us humans in some kind of reasonable perspective amidst the other forms of life that share the planet. Once, in Kenya, I spent a day in the company of an excellent field guide, studying spoor. I learned (and will never forget) to smell the difference between elephant excrement and that of a cape buffalo. Distinguishing by sight is easy: the elephant's deposit is about the size and shape of a loaf of Wonder bread; the buffalo has the plastered leavings of a large cow. But I now know that if you put your nose in the air, it's possible to tell which species has recently been in the vicinity. This is a wonderful skill I'll never be able to properly use. My more important education, however, came from another guide, a younger man named James Makau, of the East Africa Ornithological Safari. James lectured me at great length about how everybody who comes to Africa is interested in the Big Five: leopards, lions, elephants, rhinos, and buffalo. "It would be better," he advised, "if we paid more heed to the small five thousand." This is something I try to remember. The beasts of the natural world, unlike those we see on television, cannot be all celebrities; it is an integrated, mutually dependent system where the work of the smallest amoeba is critical to the ultimate survival and functioning of everything.

More and more humans are intruding on my patch of the Lake of the Woods, and they are doing so with much noise. Somebody at the resort around the bend has acquired a Sea-Doo, a "personal watercraft" that you ride like a motorcycle. Every afternoon they scream around on it out in the middle of the lake. These are the kinds of machines built to please idiots. I don't know who owns this one; I hope it is the guy I saw yesterday driving a Grand Cherokee with the vanity license plate INVESTR. I could then despise him and dismiss him twice.

The sort of young man who believes innately (though not necessarily correctly) that he'll always get the girl is the sort of fellow who buys a jet ski. The manufacturer of Sea-Doos markets them with the slogan "Everybody's Doin' It." Quite a number of people have been killed tearing around on these monsters. Though, in my quiet opinion, not enough. It's usually the wrong ones who end up paying the price for these and similar abominations. On the radio news the other morning was a report about an elderly man in his canoe being clipped by a twenty-five-foot speed boat. The canoeist was in critical condition in a hospital somewhere. The newscaster usefully told us that no one in the power boat sustained any injury.

One Sunday, in order to escape the noise along the shore, I decide to take a hike up along the power-line cut that runs north and south above the lake and the cottages. Because the trees have been taken out to accommodate maintenance of the power line, everything grows crazily here: berries, bushes, and wildflowers. I'm paying attention to flora, not fauna, typing the trees and edging off into the woods to pick a hemlock sprig for identification. I think I am alone. Suddenly, I'm startled by a sound behind me, the crack of a twig and a snorting exhalation of breath. I freeze, and turn carefully. A whitetail deer. And then a second one. They stand there and look at me as if I were a curiosity, no more harmful or dangerous than another tree. I wonder what they think. They don't run away; the opposite, in fact. As I remain perfectly still, they approach, and continue approaching until they're within about ten metres. There's a slight breeze and it is in my favour; perhaps they can't sense what I am. I risk a slight movement of my arm, a shrug, to see what will happen. That does it. Ears up, and the one closest to me gives a great snort. I've never heard deer make any other vocal sound. In a flash they are bounding off, tails high like flags on the stern of a fast boat.

I watch them disappear into the greenery and then continue on my walk. Ten minutes pass. I cover a couple of hundred metres of trail and turn a corner into another pathway where the trees are a bit larger but the forest less dense. There again, suddenly, are the deer. The same pair. Our little game of fox and goose will continue.

I'm taking what might be a sort of last look around out here. I'm in the middle of editing and finishing a film about some doctors treating AIDS in Africa. In the winter I was in Nairobi; now I'm confined to the editing suite. To be at the lake is a delicious respite. But as soon as the film is finished, I'm going to move from my long-time home in Winnipeg to faraway Toronto. Which makes me wonder whether I'll be able to keep coming back here in future summers. It will be a long journey.

One evening I luck into some quiet. The jet ski drivers are tired. Or maybe they drove their INVESTR Jeep back to the city. I snatch the opportunity to take a canoe and slip out past the breakwater that surrounds the lodge's dock. On the island that I watch from my front porch through binoculars, the eagles have nested. Their fledglings are now about three months old. Teenagers. I paddle across the open stretch of water to the cluster of white-pine populated islands, then let my canoe drift in toward the rocky shore. As the sun settles lower, the eagles comfortably occupy three of the trees, none of them the tree that holds their craggy nest. The adults eye me imperiously as I pass below them; dispassionate as Cleopatra. The youngsters, perched separately on the next two trees, not so. They set up a fuss, squawking and carrying on as if they were no better than a bunch of crows. The adults turn their heads to take this in and then, in unison, spread their great wings and lift off. They push out over the lake in the beginnings of a high circle, hunting for a late supper. The youngsters continue to squawk, bad tempered, demanding. I wonder at what age the enormous patience and dignity that characterizes their species will find its way into their bearing.

22

To Save the Planet

In the bathroom of my twelfth floor hotel room at the ITT Sheraton, sitting atop the toilet tank, is a card. The message, printed in bold letters, says, "Pitch in to save our planet!" Reading on, I learn that the way I might save the planet is to sort my towels each morning. If I do this, the housekeeping staff will launder only the ones that need it and I will "help save thousands of gallons of water and laundry detergent!" Another exclamation point.

I decide promptly to do it. Examining my towels and throwing what I've used into the tub is no trouble at all. And doing so makes me feel strangely good. Like any right-thinking – or attentive – person, I worry. How can I not? If you read the papers, listen to the news, watch TV, read magazines and books, it's impossible to not somehow believe that the planet faces imminent destruction. In all its facets, this has been the most consistently presented story of the last thirty years. A day doesn't go by without the reporting of some study or statistic or crisis or conference, or some abysmally destructive action, or protest against an abysmally destructive action.

I find the stories addictive. Like a junkie, I devour every update on the fearsome message. The accumulated opinion settles, inert, into the psyche. One of the newspapers I read is reliably alarmist: "Greenhouse effect worse than feared," declares a recent headline. Another has remained, editorially at least, sceptical, yet it too reports all the dire news.

However, as I dutifully sort my towels I become depressed. If, as the headline reports say, the world is truly going down the tubes, I'm hardly going to forestall things with a paltry gesture like this one. I'm in a room that's big enough to house six Bangladeshi families. The air conditioner roars like an arctic gale. And then I push down another palpitating panic. As I write this, I am forty-nine years old; if the world is going down the tubes, it's going down *on my watch*. And no amount of towel sorting can save me from the dread of that realization.

We humans have always altered the natural world. According to the great religions, the job was given to us as a vocation. And there have always been a number of prophets of doom to lament the impact. In 337 A.D., the Roman Tertullian wrote, "Surely it is obvious enough, if one looks at the whole world, that it is becoming daily better cultivated and more fully peopled. . . . Our teeming population is the strongest evidence our numbers are burdensome to the world which can hardly supply us from its natural elements." Seventeen hundred years later, the enormous heft of our technological power – coupled with our overwhelming numbers and soaring consumption – has made our impact on the planet unlike that of any previous humans or any other species. We are told that our activities auger profound changes in all kinds of things including climate and temperature, species balances, and CO_2 levels. The environmental writer Bill McKibbon, author of *Maybe One: A Personal and Environmental Argument for Single-Child Families*, argues that we are fast approaching the fulfillment of the desultory predictions of the Rev. Thomas Malthus who, in 1798, argued that the end of things would come from there being too many people. Our current population of six billion is a fourfold increase over the past 150 years. We enter the new millennium with *Homo sapiens* in firm, uncontested control of the planet. We are everywhere, multiplying like bad cells. Having triumphed soundly in the great primal battle, we find there is no ecological community that we have been incapable of invading and dominating. Like the CIA, our infiltration has been thorough. We are the imperialists; the rest of nature cowers before us. Richard Leakey, the Kenyan paleo-anthropologist, points out what an infinitely successful invader *Homo sapiens* is of the habitat of other species. In *The Sixth Extinction*, a 1995 discussion of bio-diversity and the impact of individual species on the ecological balance, he writes, "Mature, species-rich communities can often resist invasion attempts by most (foreign) species. But *Homo sapiens* is no ordinary species, and its attempts at invasion are almost always successful and almost always devastating for the existing community."

However, it's not only our numbers, but the size of our individual appetites that make us such a dangerous menace. We have combined choking numbers with an insatiable consumption-oriented global economy and unrelenting notions of "progress." Like Pac-Man in the old video game, we march across the landscape, chewing and devouring everything in our path. We take for granted mind-boggling levels of consumption. In hunter-gatherer times, Bill McKibbon posits, a human being consumed about 2,500 calories of energy per day, most of it food and fuel for the small fires to cook it. But the consumption of a modern North American (a guy like me who uses hotel rooms, cars, taxis, airplanes, and air conditioning) is 186,000 calories a day, most of it in the form of fossil fuel. Our rate of consumption is seventy-four times as high as our ancestors', or that of people who still live more simply than we on the earth's surface. We each consume about as much as a sperm whale.

The disturbing thing, however, is not simply how devastating the analysis we're offered is, but the ineffectiveness (and paltriness) of our response. A friend of my daughter's (they were about ten at the time), as I attempted to explain some years ago the first reports about the developing hole in the earth's ozone layer, looked at me and asked, "Well, why don't they fix it?" It was a good question. I had to explain to her that we hadn't then (and haven't now) reached the stage where we've even stopped creating the hole, let alone started to fix it.

The effect humans have on the environment of the natural world, and our worry about it, is one of the biggest issues of our times and our lives. But our response is a mess of confusing pulls and impulses. We seem to sort of know what we might do, and we're proud of that. But when it comes right down to it, we're not sure we really want to do anything at all. We know we have a responsibility, but we're not sure what that responsibility is. We know we're part of the natural world, but we're also content with the superior place we've long come to believe we inhabit.

The triumph of the scientific approach back in, say, the seventeenth century (with Descartes) augured profound changes for the emotional connection humans might have with everything else on the planet. To simply love nature became the sign of a romantic. To have credibility, one had to have analytic and quantifying credentials. In recent years, even ecology was set up as a science, and environmentalists could only gain legitimacy by joining it. Our strengths were in being dispassionate, and in being able to count.

Consequently we can know, as the World Wide Fund for Nature recently reported, that "humans have destroyed more than thirty per cent of the natural world since 1970." Nothing underlines the contradictions better than this; the thirty per cent destruction has happened since 1970. This means it occurred since the current flags went up; in the time since

Rachel Carson's and Barry Commoner's urgent warnings. In the time since the first Earth Day. What good have our knowledge and our abilities been? All our science and good-will would seem to have been ineffective.

As I write this, two great environmental disasters have weighed in on the coasts of North America. The Atlantic cod off Newfoundland in the east and salmon, sockeye, and coho in the Pacific Northwest have virtually disappeared. Five hundred years ago the cod were considered inexhaustible. Now they are gone. Surely it can't go unnoticed that these disasters transpired in the 1990s, when we have scientific means to count and predict. When there are instantaneous communication and information systems to keep us informed. When a consciousness exists that takes the health of the environment seriously and doesn't want disasters to happen. When we have a regulatory bureaucracy and a political system that possesses the machinery to take action. But still the rainforest continues to be destroyed (at twice the rate previously assumed, I recently read) while all the world's smart people are supposedly in the know. Is counting, we wonder dismally, all we're able to do?

In these paradoxical times, we mine the earth for its last resources, plug the landfills with our superfluous junk, and simultaneously make the perfunctory gesture of recycling. We are plunderers and we are tourists, innately interested in every-thing. We pursue secrets; knowledge, not mystery, is our god. Paleontologists, astronomers, molecular biologists are our heroes. Space travel, electron microscopes, nuclear telescopes and the theories of Stephen Hawking are blowing open the portals of the secrets at one end, while every newly unearthed flake of obsidian bearing some evidence of having been shaped by a human hand two million years ago blows them wide at the other. The secrets of the earth are in geology. The secrets of the universe are in astronomy. The secrets of life are in biology. The secrets of history are in archeology and palaeontology. We are engaged in rabid search.

We enthusiastically and optimistically pursue the knowledge of geology and a distant past while, *at the same time*, we are told one quarter of the earth's mammal species (not to mention countless species of plants, insects, birds, reptiles, amphibians) faces imminent risk of extinction. One great sea change has happened. The instinctive fear of nature, the oldest fear in our closet, barely exists now in active mythology; it is a quaint anachronism in our cultural mind. Even big nature doesn't scare us. We have missiles trained to demolish asteroids, should any hurtling block of rock or ice from outer space threaten the integrity of earth. Yet, we have been lucky in the fear department; we've been able to replace the fear of nature with the fear of ourselves.

Which leads us to a very unfamiliar place. What this is all about, I realize, is legacy. What's going on, as I sit in the bathroom of my air-conditioned hotel trying to decide what to do with my towels, are two things. One is a genuine trauma, a sense of helplessness (and no small hypocrisy) about the fate of the earth. The other is the equally important question of what I and my generation are doing while we have a chance, during that small moment when the world is in our hands. We pass through once; what will we leave behind? For what will we be remembered? At midlife, our preoccupations shift. I notice it all around me. A view of the world changes, subtly yet abruptly. The eye starts to cast beyond the personal to the collective or even the cosmic horizon. A switch somewhere along the way moves us from thinking solely about what's wrong with the world, to thinking about what I can do (and very soon what I did do or failed to do) to make it better. When we're young we're passionate about fixing everything that's wrong because we need to form the world into something we can live in. As we become older, we worry about what we will leave behind. My daughter and I, therefore, share certain deep concerns about the world and how it is being run. But our passions are for different reasons. What's become important to me, quite suddenly, is not just the world I must live in, but the world I'll have a hand in passing on. If I know things are wrong, to come to what is essentially the end of my shift without a profound gesture at righting them, renders me and my contemporaries the most abysmal of failures, answerable to all future generations.

The fate of the earth's environment is surely the biggest legacy issue of all. But there are others. One might be the huge disequilibrium between those of us who have and those who don't. In 1996, the holdings of the 358 billionaires who form the club of the world's richest individuals, for example, was greater than the annual income of the poorest 45 per cent of the entire world's population (almost three billion people).

The three dark clouds that have hung over the twentieth century, states writer Ryszard Kapuscinski, are racism, nationalism, and religious fundamentalism. What will happen? How will these evils grow or diminish? Who will address them? Will we hand them in a package to our children and say sorry? Or will we wrestle them to the ground yet in our lifetime? What will be the tasks and worries of our children? What should we do now?

Time is short. As more and more of it hurtles by, the sense of urgency for people like me grows. The sense of our stewardship slipping past is inextricable. If we're coming to understand anything, it's that, though we may find ways to claim whatever mess we're in as someone else's fault, we cannot say, at least for the moment, that it is somebody else's responsibility. In a short while, of course, it will be; in a short while we'll be on the sidelines and the ball will be in the hands of the next group, our children. We don't want to find ourselves over there shouting at them while knowing, with no small dismay, that our moment came and went and we did nothing.

Acknowledgements

This is the kind of book for which one's life pretty much forms the research. I'd like to acknowledge, therefore, anybody I've ever come across, known, observed, or read about who might have given me ideas or insights. More specifically, I want to extend my appreciation to many friends and acquaintances – both men and women – who, by simply sharing their lives, stories, and observations, provided fodder – sometimes unwittingly – for this book. You never know what's going to happen if you befriend a writer. Some of these people are named in the essays, others have had their names changed or been ever so slightly fictionalized. Occasionally I try to operate by Emily Dickinson's advice to "tell all the truth, but tell it slant."

I need to acknowledge a few individuals by name. Without them this book would not have happened.

Ed Knappman is not only my agent, but took a very personal interest in this topic and from the early drafts encouraged, advised, and kept me on track.

I wish to thank Doug Gibson, publisher of McClelland & Stewart, for believing in the book when it came to him as a manuscript.

And I need to acknowledge Dinah Forbes for her usual sure hand with phraseology, editing, and sharpening my paragraphs and my focus.

Lastly, I want to thank Carol Shields for her friendship, for reading the manuscript at a critical stage, and for penning her gracious introduction.